THE SKILLED TEACHER

A Systems Approach To Teaching Skills

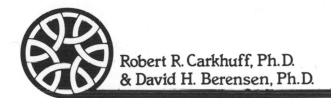

Robert R. Carkhuff, Ph.D.
& David H. Berensen, Ph.D.

with

George P. Banks, Ph.D.
Sally R. Berenson, M.S.Ed.
John R. Cannon, Ph.D.
Ted W. Friel, Ph.D.
Andrew H. Griffin, D.Ed.
Richard M. Pierce, Ph.D.
Carkhuff Institute of Human Technology

First Printing, February, 1981

Library of Congress Catalog Card No. 80-84885
International Standard Book No. 0-914234-52-8

Designed by Gail Cleare from WORDPRO, Inc., Amherst, Mass.

About the Authors

Dr. Robert R. Carkhuff, a life-long educator, is the second youngest of the hundred most-cited social scientists of our time, including such historic figures as Freud, Marx and Dewey. He is the most referenced author in counseling psychology and human resource development. Currently, Dr. Carkhuff is Chairman, Carkhuff Institute of Human Technology. He is best known as the author of three of the hundred most-cited works in the social sciences, including two volumes on **Helping and Human Relations** and **The Development of Human Resources**. He is also author of the best-selling **Art of Helping** and co-author of the **Skills of Teaching** series.

Dr. David H. Berenson is Director of Education, Carkhuff Institute of Human Technology. Teaching for more than fifteen years in elementary, secondary and higher education, Dr. Berenson has spent the last ten years revolutionizing pre-service and in-service teacher training programs. He has conducted pathfinding research in the development of effective educational systems design. Dr. Berenson is co-author of the entire **Skills of Teaching** series.

George P. Banks, Ph.D., is Director of Human Relations, Carkhuff Institute of Human Technology, and co-author of the **Multicultural Education** series.

Sally R. Berenson, M.S.Ed., is a Senior Consultant, Carkhuff Institute of Human Technology, and co-author of the **Skills of Teaching** series.

John R. Cannon is Director of Management Systems, Carkhuff Institute of Human Technology, and co-author of **The Art of Helping**.

Ted W. Friel, Ph.D., is Director of Productivity Systems, Carkhuff Institute of Human Technology, and co-author of **Toward Comprehensive Training Systems**.

Andrew H. Griffin, Ph.D., is Manager of Research, the National Education Association, and co-author of the **Multicultural Education** series.

Richard M. Pierce, Ph.D., is Director of Human Services, Carkhuff Institute of Human Technology, and co-author of **The Art of Helping**.

Other books by Robert Carkhuff available from Human Resource Development Press:

Toward Actualizing Human Potential
Art of Helping IV
Skills of Helping
Kids Don't Learn From People They Don't Like
Art of Program Development
Art of Problem Solving
Art of Health Care
Art of Developing a Career – Helper's Guide
Skills of Teaching – Content Development Skills
Skills of Teaching – Interpersonal Skills
Skills of Teaching – Teaching Delivery Skills

Preface

Who remembers the name of the first bridge builder? I know I do not! I do not think anyone else does either. Yet, there are many bridge builders and many different kinds of bridges in the world, each built to reflect the conditions and needs of the people and their contexts.

It is similar in education. If we can but learn the generic skills and knowledge, we can develop our own specific applications in the classroom. We can, each of us, become not only the implementers but the creators of our own educational technology. For just like bridge-building, educational technology begets educational technology.

What, then, are the assumptions with which we develop our educational technology? The fundamental assumption is a simple one: teachers are learners. That is not a profound assumption for anyone in education to make. However, the implications are profound.

As learners, teachers demand the same individualized learning programs that their learners demand of them. When teachers close the doors of their classrooms, they want to be uniquely themselves. They want to build "learning bridges" to their learners that reflect the uniqueness of both teachers and learners.

As learners, therefore, they require the same input into the teaching-learning process that they offer their learners. Because the teachers recognize that all learning begins with the learners' frames of reference, they insist that their own frames of reference be taken into consideration. As experts in their specialty areas, they want to influence their own learning processes.

The Skilled Teacher was created by the kind of people it is intended to serve. Teachers have provided input into the content and feedback at every stage of the book's development. They have helped to shape their own curricula.

These teachers have asked for generic teaching skills programs, which they can use to make their own unique applications. They do not want to be "programmed" to teach mechanically.

Teachers want to carry the generic skills in their hip pockets, to use them in the classroom "on their feet" to individualize their teaching deliveries; to know the generic skills that organize and guide their teaching efforts (Chapter One); to be able to develop their content and offer a learner the missing skill step or supportive knowledge (Chapter Two); to complete the organization of their content around learner exercises (Chapter Three); to employ a variety of teaching methods leading to the learners' skill application (Chapter Four); to use teaching delivery skills to set goals and develop learning programs (Chapter Five); to use interpersonal skills to personalize these goals and individualize the learning programs (Chapter Six); to understand the context of teaching systems within which the teachers make their teaching skills application (Chapter Seven).

Teachers can get what they want in **The Skilled Teacher**. They can get it because they are the real designers of this book. They will be able to become their own teachers, just as you will become your own.

The Skilled Teacher is for all teachers and would-be teachers, of all subjects, at all levels. It provides the generic skills which enable them to create their own teaching masterpieces in the classroom. It enables them to build their own bridges, their names and faces etched only in the skills and memories of the privileged learners who have had them as their teachers.

Robert R. Carkhuff, Ph.D.
David H. Berenson, Ph.D.
Amherst, Massachusetts
January, 1981

Table of Contents

The Skills
of Teaching   1

THE SOURCES OF TEACHING EFFECTIVENESS

Learning – Growing

Learning is growing. It is the opportunity to live our lives fully. It is the means by which we acquire the knowledge and skills to live, learn and work effectively. It is the meaning that we give to our lives through our physical, emotional, intellectual and social growth.

Indeed, the most significant meaning of life is growing. As learners, the only real decision which we have to make is whether or not we will grow. Whether or not we will live fully!

As the means to growth as well as the meaning of growth, learning is the greatest privilege that we will experience in life. Indeed, our learning is our life.

Teaching – Helping Others to Grow

In a related way, teaching is the opportunity to help others to live their lives fully. It is the means by which we help others to acquire the skills and knowledge to live, learn and work more effectively. It is the meaning which we help to give to our learners' lives through their physical, emotional, intellectual and social growth.

The second most significant meaning of life is helping others to grow. As teachers, the only real decision which we have to make is whether or not we will help our learners to grow. Whether we will help them to live fully or allow them to die unfulfilled.

As the source of growth, teaching is the second greatest privilege that we can experience in life. Indeed, teaching is the source of life.

Content – The Curriculum of Growth

We have already discussed two of the sources of effectiveness in teaching – the learners and the teachers. As the recipients of the learning experience, the learners bring with them the resources which we would like to help them actualize. As guides of the learning experience, we teachers bring with us the expertise to help the learners actualize their resources.

The third source of effectiveness in teaching is the content. The content to be learned is, after all, the source of learner growth and, thus, the purpose of teaching. The teacher relates to the learners through the content to be learned. The learners will come to relate to the content through the teachers who guide their learning.

The content to be learned is the content of growing. The curriculum of growth is the sum total of all learning experiences (including teachers, learners and contents) resulting in this growth. All three grow as a result of the experience.

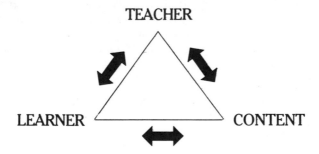

Skills – The Source of Your Effectiveness

Before you begin to learn anything about teaching skills, let us get an index of your ability to achieve goals in teaching. Simply outline the teaching skills that you would employ to accomplish your teaching goals. One way that you might organize your teaching skills is in terms of those skills involving teacher, learner and content:

Teacher: _____

_____

_____

_____

Learner: _____

_____

_____

_____

Content: _____

_____

_____

_____

At the same time that you are considering these issues, pull together any teaching programs in your special content that represent these skills. Later you may wish to examine any curriculum guides, lesson plans, teaching methods, delivery or learning programs, or any other teaching materials which you have.

There are many possible explanations which you might make to these issues concerning the skills of teaching.

If you say, "*knowing my subject area,*" you are stressing the development of your content.

If you offer, *"presenting my material,"* you are describing the organization of your content for delivery to the learners.

If you answer, *"lecturing on the content,"* you are emphasizing the methods of delivering your content to the learners.

If you indicate, *"setting learning goals,"* you are referring to the actual *delivery of the content.*

If you say, *"relating to my students,"* you are emphasizing the *interpersonal relationships* between teacher and students in the teaching/learning process.

If you noted all of the above and more, you are attending to the skills of teaching.

THE SKILLS OF TEACHING

Content Development Skills

When we think of the different sources of teaching effectiveness, we might think first of the relationship between teacher and content. This is appropriate because we prepare for our teaching by developing our content, most often before we even meet our learners.

The relationship between teachers and their content is a very significant one. The teachers' expertise with regard to their content is the basis for the teaching-learning situation, wherein a person with an extensive repertoire of responses in a particular content area shares these responses with a person with different or limited responses.

By itself, the content may make a unique contribution as a source of teaching effectiveness. However, the content is often developed in a way that does not facilitate maximum learning. For example, large percentages of the content taught at secondary and post-secondary levels emphasize facts and concepts. Such knowledge about things does not translate easily into useful skills. In contrast, when in the hands of a skillful teacher, the content can be developed in terms of both the knowledge and the skills required to facilitate learning. These teaching skills are the topics for consideration in the chapter on "Content Development Skills."

Lesson Planning Skills

As the teachers prepare for the learners, we must organize content for delivery to the learners. We must organize the content in a way that enables the learners to receive it with maximum facility.

When teachers think about organizing their content, they often think about organizing the presentation. To be sure, the presentation is the heart of the lessons they are planning. It is the moment of transmission of the content from the teacher to the learners. However, there are also stages of organizing the content that prepare the learners for the presentation. Similarly, there are stages that help to ensure that learning has taken place. These teaching skills are the topics that will be covered in the chapter on "Lesson Planning Skills."

Teaching Methods Skills

When we contemplate organizing our content in lesson plans, we must also consider the teaching methods we will employ in delivering the content. We must employ our teaching methods in such a way as to maximize learner acquisition and application of skills and knowledge.

Most often, in teaching situations, teachers emphasize didactic or pedagogic teaching methods. This is particularly true at the higher grade levels. A large percentage of secondary and post-secondary education organizes content around the lecture method. These teachers use teaching methods that tell the learners about a skill, rather than providing them with an ongoing opportunity to participate in the acquisition of that skill. But learners do not mentally record and file images of their learning if they have not had the opportunity to visually and kinesthetically exercise the skill involved. These teaching skills are the topics of the chapter on "Teaching Methods."

Teaching Delivery Skills

When we actually involve the learners in the learning process, we are employing teaching delivery skills. When we engage the learners, we are no longer teaching content. We are teaching content to learners.

Most teachers conceive of the curriculum continuing – independent of the learners. There is a daily, weekly, yearly content that must be covered. Whether or not the learners completed the last unit satisfactorily, the next unit must be introduced. The curriculum beat goes on, even if no learners hear it.

Teaching delivery skills give us an opportunity to put the learners back into the learning equation: to find out what each learner is capable of doing now and achieving later; to develop the programs that will facilitate this achievement. These teaching skills are the topics of the chapter on "Teaching Delivery Skills."

Interpersonal Skills

When we engage the learners, we must not engage them only from the external frame of reference of the content. We must also engage them from their own internal frames of reference. In some significant way, we must link the learners' internal frames of reference to the teaching goals.

In order to do this we must respond to the learners' experiences. For example, there are few teachers who ever use feeling words in relation to the learners' experiences, let alone use them accurately. How can we individualize the learners' learning programs if we cannot capture their unique experiences?

Interpersonal skills enable us to enter the learners' frames of reference: to see the learning experience through their eyes; to tailor the program to meet their unique needs. These teaching skills are the topics of the chapter on "Interpersonal Skills."

THE LEARNING PROCESS

Learning – The Basis of Teaching

Thus far, we have concentrated only upon the skills of teaching. In other words, we are developing a teacher-based system. What is important to understand is that all teaching skills must relate directly to the learners' involvement in the learning process.

For the learners, the learning process is like a voyage. The learners will be transported from one port to another. The learning experience is the ship that will transport them. And the teacher is the captain of the ship.

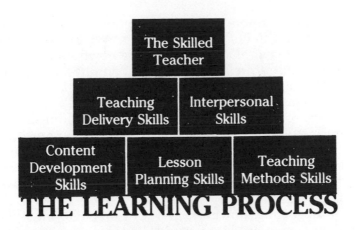

THE LEARNING PROCESS

Human Growth – A Learning Process

Before we go on to learn about the teaching skills that facilitate learning, we should understand the learning process. Human growth and development involve some kind of a gain or change in human appearance or behavior. Human learning is the process by which this gain or change occurs. In order for us to say that learning has occurred, then, there must be some kind of a demonstration of gain or change in behavior. The process out of which this learned behavior occurs can be mediated or not by human intelligence. When it is not mediated by human intelligence we say that the behavior was "conditioned." That is, the stimulus and response were associated and reinforced in such a way that either may evoke the other upon its appearance, without being processed by human intelligence.

When the behavior is mediated by intelligence, we may say that true learning has occurred. That is, the learners were involved in a learning process that enabled them to use their intelligence in describing the causes, predicting the effects and demonstrating the behavioral gain or change needed to achieve and use the effects. At the highest levels of intelligence, the learners are not only involved in such a learning process through the guidance of teachers, but also become equipped with the learning-to-learn skills they need to involve and move through the process themselves.

Human Learning – Instrumental and Conditioned

It all depends upon how we develop our human resources. To

this end, it depends upon how the environment – which is largely human –interacts with our biological selves. We can see this most clearly in the first year of a child's life. The newborn infant enters the world with little to relate to it other than physiological reflex responses. Thus, for example, the child has the sucking reflex and the palmar or grasping reflex.

If the environment is responsive to the child, these reflexes will become instrumental to the child's survival. They constitute the child's initial movements toward the world which will lead, ultimately, to his or her growth and development. The child will be able to nurse with the sucking reflex. Later on, the child will be able to grasp things with the grasping reflex.

In the beginning, however, newborn infants bring little but their inherent resources to their worlds. In their utter dependency, they wait for us to insure their survival by responding to their needs, and by gradually guiding them to the things they need to have to maintain themselves.

Habits – Conditioned Responses

One of the ways that we guide our children is by helping them to form habits. Basically, human habits are behaviors that are acquired without human intelligence. They can be acquired by associating or relating, in space and time, two or more sets of activities. At least one of these activities must satisfy some human need in order for the behavior to be repeated as a habit. For example, the child may develop the sucking habit when nourished by the mother's breast. The results may be said to be instrumental in satisfying the child's need for nourishment.

In the process, the child may develop a "conditioned" sucking response to the stimulus of the mother's nipple. In a similar manner, the child later on may develop a conditioned grasping response to the stimulus of food, which is instrumental to satisfying the child's need for nourishment. There are many other kinds of life habits which can be developed without human intelligence or intentionality.

The learning theorists write of these habits in terms of classical, instrumental, and other kinds of conditioning. The habits are "learned" only in the sense that they are repeated. They are not learned in the sense of being the product of human understanding. In fact, these habits are conditioned spinal responses, not learned responses. Indeed, most of what we teach about learning is based upon what we know about conditioning. This is precisely why we know so little about learning.

Exploration – The First Phase of Learning

Human learning and, indeed, human intelligence begin to manifest themselves when children are several months old. At this point, children begin to explore themselves and their environments. They discover the existence of and the relationships between environmental stimuli and their own responses. In other terms, the children become aware of the association of the stimuli to which they have become conditioned and the responses which have been conditioned to the stimuli. They become aware of causes and effects in their worlds.

This awareness is a two-way street. For example, the child becomes aware that the nipple or the food serves as stimulus to a sucking or grasping response. This response, in turn, will lead to satisfying a need for nourishment. The child may also become aware that a need for nourishment stimulates the response of search for the nipple or the food.

In summary, through exploring, children become aware of both their past and present relationships to their environments – including themselves. Children attempt to describe where they are in relation to themselves and the worlds around them. *Exploring* is the first stage or phase of human learning. This form of exploration begins to distinguish humankind from all other forms of life.

Understanding – The Second Phase of Learning

It is a short step from becoming aware of the ingredients of human experience to anticipating experiences. With an increasing confidence in this awareness of the relationship of stimulus and response, the child is prepared for instrumental or purposeful learning at about one year of age. In other words, the child sets out to obtain a certain result or end, independent of the means to be employed. For example, the child may set out to attract its mother, or to obtain food or an object that is out of reach.

Drawing from this awareness of the relationship between stimulus and response or cause and effect, the child sets a goal of achieving certain effects. The goals of the instrumental act are often only seen later although some approximation of them was obviously intended from the beginning.

In summary, children understand their relationships to future events or experiences. They are, in effect, attempting to predict the consequences of their efforts. They understand where they want to be in their worlds. This *understanding* is the second stage or phase of human learning. It is what allows humankind to anticipate its future – another distinction from other forms of life.

Action – The Third Phase of Learning

The next phase of human learning flows naturally from the understanding phase. It involves the development of behavioral patterns instrumental to achieving goals. From the end of the first year onwards, the child draws from his or her repertoire of behaviors to produce the responses needed to achieve a goal. For example, the child may laugh or cry to bring the mother or surrogate to him or her. The child may move his or her hand in the direction of the unreachable food or object. There may be a series of trial and error experiences. These experiences may either confirm the child's responses, through reaching the goal and experiencing satisfaction, or else they may reject the child's responses, through not reaching the goal.

In summary, children begin to act in order to get from where they are to where they want to be within their worlds. They are, in effect, attempting to control themselves and their worlds. *Acting* is the third stage or phase of learning. It enables human beings to plan and work towards the end of influencing their future.

Human Growth – A Learning Prototype

The first year of human development serves as a prototype for all human learning. The child's reflexes are unknowingly conditioned as habitual responses to certain stimuli. These habits serve as the limited repertoire of responses with which the child initially approaches the world. Improvement in the quantity and quality of responses with which the learner ultimately relates to the world depends upon the development of the child's intelligence. This, in turn, depends upon how effectively he or she goes through the stages or phases of learning.

Initially, the child explores and identifies the nature of the stimuli and responses in his or her experience. Transitionally, the child comes to understand the interactive nature of stimuli and responses, anticipates the effects of one upon the other and develops goals to achieve these effects. Finally, the child acts by drawing from his or her developing repertoire of responses to attempt to achieve goals. The child's action behavior is shaped by feedback or by the effects it achieves. This feedback recycles the stages or phases of learning as the child explores more extensively, understands more accurately and acts more effectively. This ascending, enlarging spiral of exploration, understanding and action is the source of the adult's improving repertoire of responses.

What goes on in the first year of life goes on in more and more refined ways throughout life – or not. How effectively we live our lives depends totally upon how efficiently and effectively we learn.

The Skills of Exploring – An Intuitive Activity

Just watch the learners' exploratory activities. Perhaps we can see these in a classroom most clearly in the absence of formal teaching. The learners may become interested in some object or mechanism on their own initiative in the absence of a teacher. The learners will approach the material or object and position themselves so as to give it their attention. They may observe the thing for a while, perhaps listen to it and then probably touch it. The touching will lead to handling. The learners may try it out in different ways, turning the material around or over, or attaching it to other things.

The learners may try to figure out what the thing is and does, and maybe even why and how it does it. Finally, they may try to do whatever it does. In the process, they have found out what they know about it, and what they can do with it. In short, they have found out where they are in relation to the learning experience. (So have their teachers, if they are present.)

The learners must address all sources of learning in a similar manner. If the teacher is presenting some content in the classroom, the learners must use all of their exploring skills to address the teacher, the content, the delivery or method, and the classroom environment as dimensions of the learning experience. Learners must also address themselves as potential sources of learning, in terms of the learning experiences and learning skills that they bring to the learning process. By exploring all dimensions of the learning experience, the learners can find out where they are in relation to the learning experience. They will then be ready to find out where they want to be.

The Skills of Understanding – A Mediating Activity

The learners may engage in a series of understanding activities. They may relate the dimensions of their current experiences to those of their past experiences. They may organize the dimensions of these experiences in different ways based upon their similarities and differences. The learners may organize the dimensions of the learning experience in still different ways based upon their functions and the values of these functions to their learning. The learners may generalize their needs from these values, and set generalized learning goals based upon the learning experience and specific learning objectives derived from the different dimensions of the learning experience. Or they may do all of this, by simply determining what, of all the content possible, they have yet to learn.

Where there is a teacher with a teaching goal, all of these activities can take place in relation to the teaching goal. The learners may set their learning objectives in relation to the teaching goals. Where there is no teacher, the learners may set their learning objectives based upon their generalized needs. In summary, the learners gain increasing confidence in their understanding of where they are in relation to where they want to be. They are ready to act in order to get there.

The Skills of Acting – A Culminating Activity

Observing the learner in the action phase reveals the types of activities in which learners engage. First, they work to master the knowledge and skills involved in the learning goals. If the teachers have established the goal, they learn the knowledge or skills the teachers have developed. If teachers are not involved, learners can begin to define their skills objectives in terms of the deficits or problems they are having in achieving their goals, and to develop and implement programs designed to achieve those objectives.

In either event, having acquired the learning, the learners can repeat or practice the skill involved until it is readily and effectively available to them. Then they can apply it, either in some way that was intended by the teacher, or that is relevant to their own experience. They can continue to apply it in real-life, everyday living, learning, playing and working experiences. Finally, they can transfer the learning to unique and creative situations in their lives. This is the culmination of mastery; to be able to create with what you have learned.

Human Learning – A Growth Process

The learning voyage, then, begins where the learners are. Before our learners can embark upon their learning journeys, they must be able to identify the degrees of longitude and latitude at their points of origin. In terms of the learning process, they must know precisely where they are in relation to the learning experience. In order to do this, they must explore where they are. Learner exploration is the first phase of learning.

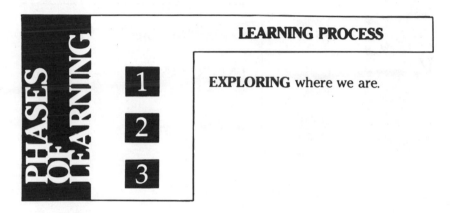

When the learners know where they are, then they can determine their ports of destination. They must know the degrees of longitude and latitude of their objectives. In terms of the learning process, the learners must understand where they are in relation to where they want to be, and also what they will need to obtain from the learning experience in order to get there. Learner understanding is the second phase of learning.

Finally, when the learners have established their ports of

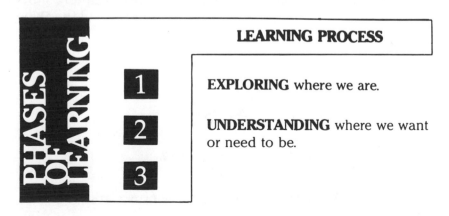

destination clearly in mind, they can begin their learning voyages. When they understand where they are in relation to where they want to be, they can act in order to get there. In other words, they can develop their own individualized learning processes, designed to achieve their learning objectives. Learner *acting* is the third phase of learning.

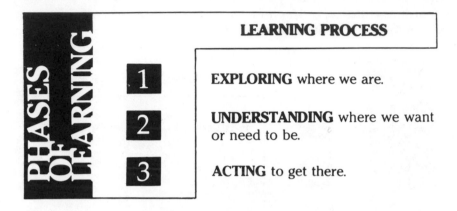

Teaching – The Basis of Learning

The teacher is the captain of the ship which transports the learners from port to port. All of the captain's skills must, therefore, relate directly to the passengers' welfare.

Everything the teacher does must directly facilitate the learners' movement through the learning process. At all stages of learning the teacher must be guided by what is effective for the learner. In the end, the teachers' effectiveness will be determined by their ability to facilitate the learners' recycling of learning in a life-long learning process. How the teaching skills relate directly to learners' movement through the learning process is the exciting topic of **The Skilled Teacher**.

RESEARCH BACKGROUND: THE SKILLS OF TEACHING

The Problem of Limited Variability

The evidence indicating that all helping and human relationships may be "for better or worse" is extensive. That is, relationships between supposedly "more knowing" and "less knowing" persons may have facilitative *or* retarding effects upon the latter. These relationships include husband-wife, parent-child, teacher-student, counselor-counselee, therapist-client, health care provider-patient and even employer-employee relationships (Anthony, 1978; Aspy and Roebuck, 1977; Carkhuff, 1969, 1971; Gage, 1977).

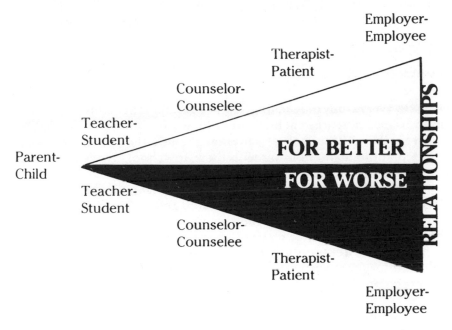

For this data we can appeal to the hard evidence of programmatic research, or to common sense. Each of us has experienced school years in which we have flourished in our growth and development under the leadership of one teacher; a time when we were able to do things that we were previously unable to do. Conversely, we have each experienced years in which we have been retarded or even deteriorated in our development under the direction of another teacher; a time when we were unable to do things that we were previously able to do.

If we reflect upon it, we will probably recall three or four teachers who were facilitative and four or five who were retarding. One of the greatest indictments against teaching is that the majority of our teachers did not make a difference. We cannot even remember their names and faces now.

This great horde of neutral teachers with neutral effects points out one of the major problems involved in researching education.

15

There is not enough variability in most teachers' levels of functioning to discriminate the sources of teaching effectiveness and, thus, to determine the relative effects of schooling upon learner achievement. If we select teachers at random, in all probability, most of them will be teachers who do not make a difference. So we end up getting essentially neutral or negative results. The limited variability in teachers leads directly to a second major research problem: the amount of variability that the school currently accounts for, perhaps in part because of the essential neutrality of many teachers.

Learner Variables

In every study of teaching, learner variables account for more of the variance in learner achievement than all of the school variables put together. These learner variables include the pre-instructional skills that the learners bring with them to school, as well as family processes and home background factors.

Pre-instructional learner variables include intelligence quotients (IQs), scholastic aptitudes and pre-tested achievement. Historically, the learner's scholastic aptitude or prior achievement, measured before the beginning of instruction, relates most highly to learner achievement after teaching. These results appear whether the teaching lasts for fifteen minutes or a whole school year. The correlations of preinstructional variables with postinstructional achievement range as high as .7 to .9 (Gage, 1977).

Therefore, many investigators have indicated that there is little variance in achievement remaining to be accounted for after pre-instructional variables are considered. They argue that the total importance of teaching is "inherently trivial" (Heath and Nielson, 1974). However, it is a misinterpretation to conclude that teaching per se makes little difference. Indeed, none of the studies that have been conducted have compared teaching and no teaching.

Most important, the preinstructional variables against which schooling variables have been compared represent the outcome of years of experience and development. During these years, learner ability and achievement have been influenced by significant environmental variables: many teachers in the form of parents and surrogates, friends and peers, as well as the influence of mass media, the neighborhoods, shopping centers and the like. Indeed, the effects of the home and community relative to the school are directly proportional to time spent in each context, rather than the potency of each environment.

Family Processes and Home Background

In his historic study, Coleman (1966) found that family processes and home background predominantly accounted for the learners' contributions to learning. The family processes alone, including the level of expectations, aspirations and beliefs regarding the importance of work for life, along with stimulation and support, contribute twenty-two percent of the variability in student achievement. The home background alone, including socioeconomic conditions, family structure and racial and ethnic group membership, contributes five percent to the measures of learner achievement.

School and Home Interactions

When the family processes and home backgrounds interact with each other and the schools, the results are revealing. Together, the family processes and home background contribute twenty-one percent of the variance in student achievement. Home background in interaction with the schools contributes another twenty-one percent. Finally, the three variables in interaction with each other contribute still another twenty-one percent.

These results indicate that learner variables, by themselves, appear to be the dominant source of student achievement. While schools, by themselves, contribute only five percent of the variability in learner achievement, in interaction with the family processes and home background the school becomes a potent source of effect, contributing nearly fifty percent of the variability. Indeed, the school can only be seen as a potent force when viewed in interaction with the various influences of home and community.

These community influences must be taken into consideration in the planning and design of the teaching curricula, as well as in the training and development of the teacher. It is within the learners' home and family context that teaching takes place. It is to this community context that teaching must be responsive in order to be pre-potent with regard to the other far-ranging sources of retardation that impinge upon learner development. Within this multi-cultural context the school can respond fully to the learners' needs (Griffin, 1977; Jones, 1977; McCune, 1977; Pierce, 1977).

The Effects of Schooling

In addition to the potency of learner variables, there is good reason that the school has historically had little effect upon learner achievement. Most of the things that happen in school are unrelated to learner achievement. Certainly, the organization and the administrative practices of the school have questionable effects. On the other hand, certain characteristics of the teachers and their content are potential sources of effect, especially when strengthened by information derived from studies of facilitative teachers (Berenson, 1977; Gage, 1977; Kaya, et al, 1967).

How the School is Organized

The school organization or contextual variables have no effect upon learning. Thus, the effects of grouping practices based upon student needs, class size, achievement grouping, teaming, open classrooms and individualized instruction are neutral. Scheduling practices like block scheduling, core scheduling, modular scheduling, flexible scheduling, dual progress and the Joplin plan have no effect. Personnel utilization programs involving differentiated staffing, specialization, paraprofessionalization and pre- and inservice preparation yield nothing. General programming practices built around team teaching, cooperative teaching, self-contained teaching and departmental teaching have no relationship to student benefits. Indeed, the impact of innovation upon learner achievement is negative:

> . . . the impact of level of innovation was negative – that is, the greatest educational growth (in reading and artithmetic achievement during the third grade) occurred in programs with a more moderate emphasis on innovation; . . . (furthermore) the consistent overachievers actually tended to be members of programs with a lower level of innovation . . . (American Institutes for Research, 1976, p. 14).

In the total research, the findings are contradictory and self-neutralizing.

The Impact of the School Administration

Furthermore, the school administrator does not prove to be a potent source of effect in student learning. The administrator's traits and characteristics, including his or her demographic characteristics, preparation for decision-making, work production and need structure are unrelated to learning. The administrator's background and knowledge, including ratings, training and experience, salaries and even cooperative administration have no yield. The administrator's styles and climates, from open, laissez-faire and familiar; through democratic, business-like and responsible; to autocratic, closed and controlling, do not affect student learning. The only time the administrator has been found to be a potent source of effect upon student learning is when the administrator is trained in the same skills (for example, interpersonal skills) as the teachers. Thus, the administrator can serve not only as model and agent for the teachers' gain in functioning but also as reinforcer for the translation of this change to student benefits (Aspy and Roebuck, 1978; Cannon and Friel, 1977).

Teacher Variables

Even when we enter the classroom to study the direct effects of the teachers upon learners, we find that many teacher characteristics do not make a difference. Teachers' demographic characteristics, such as sex, race, age and marital status, are all unrelated to learner outcomes. The teachers' background and experience, including the effects of their preservice and inservice training, content knowledge and degree of specialization, are negative with regard to student learning. The teachers' attitudes and personalities, including whether the teachers are warm and flexible, turbulent or fearful, business-like or stimulating, even matching teacher personality to learner personality, are all wanting as sources of student learning.

What about teachers is effective, then? The teachers' role functions and classroom behaviors, including their modes and methods of presenting! Teachers who are responsive to student needs, flexible in their presentations and varied in their methods are most effective in producing student achievement. They employ varied methodologies to deliver content, derived at least in part from the students' needs and frames of reference. All of this must be done in a context that is completely committed to facilitating the students' acquisition of skills.

The truth, then, is that what the teachers do behaviorally and not who they are demographically is what makes a difference in learning. Let us take a look at some of the programs the teachers deliver.

The Effects of Curriculum

If teachers are responsive, flexible and varied in their presentations, what do they present? All dimensions of the curricula are important. These dimensions include: cognitive processing; operationalization and organization of content; sources of instruction; teaching delivery; and, interpersonal dimensions including reinforcements.

In terms of cognitive processing, students improve on all measures of learning when presented with learning material oriented to reflect the properties of learning. These properties include process orientation, style and level of learning, creativity and structure and direction. In other words, teaching curricula that incorporate the naturalistic learning patterns found in the learners' experiential exploration, personalized understanding and behavioral action is most effective in facilitating learner growth and development.

The operationalization of the content is also an important source of effect. The ability to define the skills content in measurable performance objectives is critical. The ability to break out the skill steps involved in achieving the objectives is necessary. The ability to mobilize the knowledge necessary to teach the skill objective is also supportive.

The sequencing or organizing of the content for delivery is another important factor. The mode, direction and rate of learning must be related to an overview and delivery of the skills to be applied. The sequencing methods, including contingency, simple-to-complex, concrete-to-abstract and immediate-to-remote must also be related to the students' abilities and perceptions.

The sources of instruction or teaching methods are also crucial for student learning. When subject matter is presented through a variety of sensory modalities, it significantly relates to measures of student growth. Effective curricula must be presented in operational step-by-step procedures via auditory, visual and kinesthetic modes from a wide variety of sources. The kinesthetic learning must be emphasized.

Delivery of the skills content involves the teacher in directly affecting the learning process. Atomistic programming is the conclusion of the delivery. It must be based upon extremely fine diagnoses of students' abilities; goals must be set that are related to these abilities; programs must be developed and monitored to achieve these goals. The knowledge and skills content must move through a continuum from classroom acquisition, through application to transfer into life experiences. In a preferred sequence, learning must successively approximate reality.

Finally, the interpersonal dimensions, including reinforcement, are relevant to student benefits. All dimensions of curriculum development and delivery must begin and end with the learners' frames of reference. All effective curricula must be developed to incorporate an explicit way of determining accuracy, including relevant knowledge of results, time and practice. The truth, then, is that what the teachers do, and the curricula they deliver, are the significant sources of effect in learner achievement.

The Principles of Effectiveness

Some of the models of teaching are helpful, if not comprehensive, in pointing up the effective ingredients of teaching effectiveness (Joyce, 1978; Joyce and Weil, 1972). All models translate their mission in terms of content objectives. Some of the models focus programmatically upon the preparation of the skills and knowledge of the content (Aspy and Roebuck, 1977; Bloom, et al, 1956; Kratwohl, 1964; Metfessel, Michael and Kirsner, 1969; Payne, 1968).

Most models of teaching emphasize the teaching delivery that takes place between teachers and learners. These deliveries are calculated to accomplish one of three objectives: growth in academic skills, for learning ways of dealing with intellectual complexities (Ausubel, 1963; Bruner, Goodnow and Austin, 1967; Lorayne and Lucas, 1974; Piaget, 1952; Sigel, 1969; Sullivan, 1967; Taba, 1967); growth in intrapersonal skills and knowledge, for individual problem-solving (Glasser, 1969; Gordon, 1961; Hunt, 1970; Perls, Hefferline and Goodman, 1977; Rogers, 1951, 1969; Schutz, 1967); or, growth in interpersonal skills and knowledge, for group problem-solving (Aspy and Roebuck, 1977; Benne, Gibb and Bradford, 1964; Dewey, 1916; Massialas and Cox, 1966; Michaelis, 1963; Mosston, 1972; Oliver and Sharrer, 1968; Shaftel and Shaftel, 1967; Thelen, 1960).

One way of utilizing these models is to employ their concepts of the effective ingredients of teaching in studying those facilitative teachers who have a potently positive effect. We can then teach the skills they possess to the teachers with a neutral or even retarding effect. When we do this, we find that there are certain characteristics of the teachers and their contents that extend the research yields. Let us try to summarize these learnings from facilitative teachers, in the form of learning principles.

1. In involving the learners in learning, effective teachers develop learning experiences which incorporate the process orientation, style, creativity, structural and functional properties of learning: all learning involves the naturalistic patterns found in experiential ex-

ploration, personalized understanding and behavioral action.

2. In developing the content, effective teachers operationalize the content in skills, and break out its achievement in steps and supportive knowledge: all effective content culminates in a skill objective.

3. In organizing the content, effective teachers develop learner responsive sequencing that begins with an image of skill application and concludes in the reality of skill application: all effective content is organized around the skill application.

4. In developing the teaching methods, effective teachers present the skills content through a variety of sensory modalities, especially kinesthetic: all effective teaching methods emphasize kinesthetic learning activities.

5. In delivering the skills content, effective teachers make moment-to-moment diagnoses of the learners' needs in terms of the skills content, and develop the resultant atomistic programming to meet these needs: all effective teaching delivery is broken down into atomistic steps.

6. Finally, in relating to the learners, effective teaching involves the moment-to-moment individualizing of programs in terms of the learners' internal frames of reference: all effective learning begins with the learners' frames of reference.

Summary of Research Findings

As with all other human relationships, teaching can clearly have either facilitative or retarding effects. Indeed, the learner preinstructional levels of functioning are a product of the previous relationships that learners have had with other "teachers" in their homes and communities.

Whether the effects of teaching are facilitative or retarding depends upon the level of the teachers' skills. Do they have the skills to develop their content according to a skill objective? To organize the content around the skill application? To teach the content emphasizing kinesthetic learning experiences? To deliver the content with atomistic programming? To relate to the learners with responsive interpersonal skills? These are the skills that high-level functioning teachers have, and that other teachers need to learn.

Depending upon whether or not the teachers have these skills, the teachers will have different effects upon learner achievement: high levels of impact accounting for an increasingly large amount of variance in student learning, alone and intentionally in interaction with learner variables, including family and home variables; low levels of impact with continuing neutral effects, alone and only inadvertently with learner variables.

When the door to the classroom is closed, there are only the teachers, the learners and the content. The teacher is the critical ingredient in accounting for additional amounts of learning achievement. How well the teacher implements teaching skills in developing and delivering the content will determine the potential for student achievement. How well the teachers respond to student needs and prepare the students to receive the teachers' contributions will determine how well the students learn.

References

American Institutes for Research. *Impact of Educational Innovation on Student Performance.* Palo Alto, Cal.: American Institutes for Research, 1976.

Anthony, W.A. *The Principles of Psychiatric Rehabilitation:* Amherst, Mass.: Human Resource Development Press, 1978.

Aspy, D.N. and Roebuck, Flora N. *Kids Don't Learn from People They Don't Like.* Amherst, Mass.: Human Resource Development Press, 1977.

Ausubel, D. *Psychology of Meaningful Verbal Learning.* New York, N.Y.: Grune and Stratton, 1963.

Benne, K., Gibb, J.R. and Bradford, L. *T-Group Theory and Laboratory Method.* New York, N.Y.: Wiley, 1964.

Berenson, D.H. "The Effective Ingredients of Education," in *Toward Excellence in Education*, R. R. Carkhuff and J. W. Becker. Amherst, Mass.: Carkhuff Institute of Human Technology, 1977.

Bloom, B.S., Englehart, M.D., Furst, E.J., Hill, W.H. and Kratwohl, D.R. *A Taxonomy of Educational Objectives: Handbook I, The Cognitive Domain.* New York, NY: Longmans, Green, 1956.

Bruner, J., Goodnow, J. J. and Austin, G. A. *A Study of Thinking.* New York, N.Y.: Science Editions, Inc., 1967.

Cannon, J. and Friel, T. W. "The Administrator in the Learning Equation," in *Toward Excellence in Education*, R. R. Carkhuff and J. W. Becker. Amherst, Mass.: Carkhuff Institute of Human Technology, 1977.

Carkhuff, R. R. *Helping and Human Relations.* New York, N.Y.: Holt, Rinehart & Winston, 1969.

Carkhuff, R. R. *The Development of Human Resources.* New York, N.Y.: Holt, Rinehart & Winston, 1971.

Coleman, J. S. *Equality of Educational Opportunity.* Washington, D.C.: U.S. Government Printing Office, 1966.

Dewey, J. *Democracy and Education.* New York, N.Y.: MacMillan, 1916.

Gage, N. L. *The Scientific Basis of the Art of Teaching.* New York, N.Y.: Teachers College Press, 1977.

Glasser, W. *Schools Without Failure.* New York, N.Y.: Harper & Row, 1969.

Gordon, W. *Synectics.* New York, N.Y.: Harper & Row, 1961.

Griffin, A. H. "A Human Technology for Community Justice," in *Toward Excellence in Education*, R. R. Carkhuff and J. W. Becker. Amherst, Mass.: Carkhuff Institute of Human Technology, 1977.

Heath, R. W. and Nielson, M. A. "The Research Basis for Performance Based Teacher Education." *Review of Educational Research* 44:463-483.

Hunt, D. E. "A Conceptual Level Matching Model for Coordinating Learner Characteristics with Educational Approaches." *Interchange, OISE Research Journal 1*, June, 1970.

Jones, M. "The Learner in the Learning Equation," in *Toward Excellence in Education*, R. R. Carkhuff and J. W. Becker. Amherst, Mass.: Carkhuff Institute of Human Technology, 1977.

Joyce, B. R. *Selected Learning Experiences.* Washington, D.C.: Association for Supervision and Curriculum Development, 1978.

Joyce, B. R. and Weil, M. *Models of Teaching.* Englewood Cliffs, N.J.: Prentice Hall, 1972.

Kaya, E., Gerhard, M., Stasiewski, A. and Berenson, D. H. *Developing a Theory of Educational Practices for the Elementary School.* Norwalk, Conn.: Ford Foundation Fund for the Improvement of Education, 1967.

Kratwohl, D. R. "The Taxonomy of Educational Objectives: Its Use in Curriculum Building," in *Defining Education Objectives*, C. M. Lindvall, ed. Pittsburgh, Pa.: University of Pittsburgh Press, 1964.

Lorayne, H. and Lucas, J. *The Memory Book.* New York, N.Y.: Ballantine, 1974.

Massialas, B. and Cox, B. *Inquiry in Social Studies.* New York, N.Y.: McGraw-Hill, 1966.

McCune, S. "The Teacher in the 'Learning Equation," in *Toward Excellence in Education*, R.R. Carkhuff and J. W. Becker. Amherst, Mass.: Carkhuff Institute of Human Technology, 1977.

Metfessel, N. S., Michael, W. B. and Kirsner, D. A. "Instrumentation of Bloom's and Kratwohl's Taxonomies for the Writing of Educational Objectives." *Psychology in the Schools* 7:227-231.

Michaelis, J. U. *Social Studies for Children in Democracy.* Englewood Cliffs, N.J.: Prentice Hall, 1963.

Mosston, M. *Teaching: From Command to Discovery.* Belmont, Cal.: Wadsworth Publishing Co., 1972.

Oliver, D. and Shaver, J. *Teaching Public Issues in the High School.* Boston, Mass.: Blaisdell Publishing Co., 1968.

Payne, D. A. *The Specification and Measurement of Learning Outcomes.* Waltham, Mass.: Blaisdell Publishing Co., 1968.

Perls, F., Hefferline, R. and Goodman, P. *Gestalt Therapy: Excitement and Growth in the Human Personality.* New York, N.Y.: Crown, 1977.

Pierce, R. M. "The Parent in the Learning Equation," in *Toward Excellence in Education*, R.R. Carkhuff and J. W. Becker. Amherst, Mass.: Carkhuff Institute of Human Technology, 1977.

Piaget, J. *The Origins of Intelligence in Children.* New York, N.Y.: International University Press, 1952.

Rogers, C. R. *On Becoming a Person.* Boston, Mass.: Houghton Mifflin, 1951.

Rogers, C. R. *Freedom to Learn.* Columbus, Ohio: Merrill, 1969.

Schaftel, F. and Schaftel, G. *Role-Playing for Social Values: Decision-Making in the Social Studies.* Englewood Cliffs, N.J.: Prentice Hall, 1967.

Schutz, W. Joy. *Expanding Human Awareness.* New York, N.Y.: Grove Press, 1967.

Sigel, I. E. "The Piagetian System and the World of Education," in *Studies in Cognitive Development*, D. Elkind and J. Flavell, eds. New York, N.Y.: Oxford, 1969.

Sullivan, E. *Piaget and the School Curriculum: A Critical Appraisal.* Toronto: Ontario Institute for Studies in Education, 1967.

Taba, H. *Teacher's Handbook for Elementary Social Studies.* Reading, Mass.: Addison-Wesley, 1967.

Thelen, Herbert A. *Classroom Grouping for Teachability.* New York, N.Y.: Wiley, 1967.

Content
Development Skills   **2**

DEVELOPING EFFECTIVE CONTENT

Experiences You Have Had With Content

We have all, as learners, had experience with classroom content. We had to memorize and recite facts in history. We discussed many concepts of the human condition in social studies. We learned principles of science in our science courses. We applied mathematical skills in math.

Unfortunately, in few courses did we get both the skills and the supportive knowledge that make skills learning possible. Often, when we learned a skill we were not exposed to the supportive knowledge. And when we learned the knowledge, we were not taught the operational skill.

For example, this might even take place in areas of physical skills. We might learn to throw a ball without learning the principle of facing and stepping toward the person to whom we are throwing the ball (the ball tends to go where the body faces). Consequently, many of us wound up throwing the ball across our bodies and never reached the target with accuracy or sufficient velocity.

The Principle of Content Development

Similarly, we were often taught only the facts and concepts, and not how to translate them into skills. For example, our teachers or coaches told us to throw the ball "harder" or "more accurately," but they did not teach us the skills that would enable us to operationalize these concepts.

Most often we were frustrated because we could not handle many of the different learning applications that were asked of us. We wanted to, but we did not know how to translate the knowledge into skills, or how to support the skills with knowledge.

It is clear that both skills and knowledge are necessary for a comprehensive and functional content. Confidence comes from doing what we know and knowing what we do. But, above all, confidence comes from our competence in the performance of the skill objective defined by our knowledge and skills. In this context, the fundamental principle of content development is relevant: *all effective content culminates in a skill objective.* This is the topic of the following chapter.

Teaching Preparation

As teachers, we will find an exciting relationship in our lives with our content. Internally, our content is what makes us enthusiastic about our lives. Its broad-ranging knowledge expands our horizons of learning. It is what makes us learners. Indeed, our content is what makes us *full of life.*

Externally, our content is what makes us enthusiastic about the lives of others, about sharing knowledge and transmitting our own personal commitments to teaching. It is what makes us teachers. Indeed, our content is what makes us *givers of life.*

Developing our content is the first step in preparing to share our content with our learners. Development of our content is the first step in preparing to share our *lifefulness* with our learners.

An Index of Your Content Development

As teachers, we have all had a lot of experience with developing our content. Right? Wrong! Even experienced teachers look for direction from supervisors and administrators. The content may take the form of a detailed outline including goals and objectives. It may simply entail the use of a textbook series or a particular type of curriculum. Most times, the decision of what content to teach is made on the basis of past experience. "We'll teach the same content this year as we did last year."

Before we learn to develop our content, let us ask ourselves the essential question about our content: "What is it that we wish to share?" Or, put another way, "What are the most important dimensions of our content?" You may wish to record these responses for future reference.

_____

_____

_____

_____

_____

At this point, it may also be helpful for you to get an index of our previous learning about content development. Perhaps you can take some aspect of our specialty content and outline how you would develop the dimensions you have just noted in order to maximize student learning. You may think this through or use the space below for your notes. Be sure to draw upon all of your previous learning with regard to content development.

_____

_____

_____

_____

_____

The Dimensions of Content

If we seriously attempt to develop any content, there are many questions which we must raise. These questions concern the important dimensions of the content which we wish to teach our learners:

Is it the *knowledge* that we are trying to share with our learners? The knowledge that will help them to identify certain aspects of their own worlds and what is going on in them!

Or is it the *skills* that we are trying to teach? So that our learners can act effectively in their worlds!

Or perhaps it is some kind of a positive learning *attitude* toward our content which we wish to instill in our learners? So that our learners can involve themselves in a life-long learning process!

Maybe it is a combination of knowledge and skills and attitudes that enables our learners to proceed effectively, making sense out of and acting upon with confidence the wondrous maze of experiences we call life.

Now take a look at your outline of how you would use your content development skills in preparing your specialty content. The critical question is this: have you included operational steps for implementing your concepts of content development? If so, you will be able to prepare your content effectively. If not, you will have to learn to develop the content of the skills involved.

Levels of Knowledge

Before we can determine what we want to transmit to our learners, we need to understand different kinds of conceptual development. The first kind of conceptual development involves *knowledge* or what we understand *about* things.

At the first level of conceptual development, then, *facts* identify what people, places or things are involved in the learning objective. They tell us what things are.

At the second level of conceptual development, *concepts* tell us something about the facts. They tell us what things do.

At the third level of conceptual development, *principles* explore how and why things do what they do, why they are important, and when and where to use the things.

Discrimination and Communication

By themselves, these levels of knowledge allow us to make *discriminations* about the presence or absence of things and what they do. Indeed, the very foundation of our treasured freedom in the Western world is based upon our knowledge or ability to make these discriminations.

These levels of knowledge also enable us to *communicate* about things by knowing their names and functions. In other words, we can share our discriminations with others and, thus, free them to make choices in their worlds.

Levels of Skills

Clearly, knowledge about something does not necessarily enable us to *do* something. Because we understand what a thing is and does and even why to use it, does not mean that we can do the things involved in a learning objective. For example, as teachers, we now know *about* teaching preparation skills, but we do not know how to *do* or implement the things involved in preparing for teaching.

We can only achieve the learning objective when we have the *skills* to perform it. Skills constitute the second kind of conceptual development. Skills are a series of steps that we perform or do. They are summarized in an action or behavioral response. That is to say, they are manipulatable, observable and measurable. In this context, skills are achievable and repeatable and, therefore, teachable.

There are two additional levels of conceptual development that enable us to learn and apply skills.

The fourth level of conceptual development involves the *skill objectives* which tell us what we want our learners to be able to do.

The fifth level of conceptual development involves developing the *skill steps* which we need to implement or achieve the skill objectives.

Application & Transfer – Uses of Skills

In summary, skills define our exercise of freedom. In conjunction with the fine discriminations based upon our knowledge about things in our worlds, skills enable us to act in a multitude of ways. For example, we can apply our teaching skills to the many different situations in which we have been taught to apply them.

In addition, skills can be transferred in ways that we have not been taught. We can put our skills together in combinations and make applications that were previously unknown to us. For example, we can transfer our teaching skills to other human relationships such as parenting, helping or managing others.

In short, our skills constitute our repertoire of growth responses to life. They are the resources with which we march forward to claim our essential humanity. The extensiveness and intensity – the quantity and quality – of our repertoire of skills is the only thing that separates us from other forms of life. Indeed, defined as the application and transfer of behavioral responses, skills define learning and thus, life.

Uses of Skills

There is an order involved in developing our content. We must first define our skill objective. The skill objective will tell us where we are going, i.e., what the learners need to be able to do. This definition will enable us to proceed efficiently in constructing our content.

The skill objective will also enable us to develop our skill steps. The skill steps define what the learners need to be able to do in order to achieve the skill objective.

The skill steps will allow us to define the knowledge needed to support the achievement of the skill objective. Each step is examined to see what the learner needs to know about the operations involved; what things are involved in doing the skill (facts); what these things mean and what they do (concepts); and why, when and where the skill steps are done (principles).

Together, the skill steps and supportive knowledge will make it possible to achieve the skill objective of the content. Ultimately, the skills-building process will make it possible for us to achieve any goal.

These are the topics of the content development skills building section that follows.

DESIGNING SKILL OBJECTIVES

Identifying Skills – A Profound Operation

The most profound level of content to contemplate is the skill

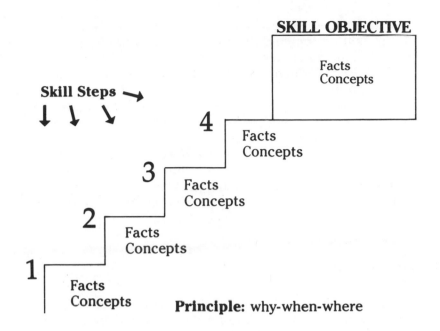

SKILL OBJECTIVE

Facts
Concepts

Skill Steps →

↓ ↓ ↘

4
Facts
Concepts

3
Facts
Concepts

2
Facts
Concepts

1
Facts
Concepts

Principle: why-when-where

objective. From the largest possible perspective, developing a skill objective is the first step toward achieving any goals in our lives. The skill objective makes it possible for us to define goals in achievable terms. It makes "throwing out a sky hook" and "picking ourselves up by our own bootstraps" literally and physically possible.

For example, when NASA's Dr. John Houbolt developed the objective of the lunar-orbit rendezvous, he separated the lunar landing mission into precise functions. Thus, he operationalized putting a person on the moon – a product of humankind's most vivid imagination. If we can put a person on the moon with the systems and technology of skills objectives, can we do less for our learners in our classrooms here on earth?

Teaching Learners To Do

Our skill objective is a statement of what our learners will be able to do when they complete the skill steps. As such, our skill objective constitutes the end result of learning. In other words, our skill objective is the goal of learning. Unfortunately, much of our classroom content does not qualify as the achievement of skill objectives.

For example, writing a list of words or phrases or dates from memory, or labeling a diagram are not skills objectives in the true sense of the phrase. There are, to be sure, skills involved: the skill of recall; the skill of copying. If those skills are what you want your learners to learn, then make them the learning objectives and teach them. But these may not be the skills that we want our learners to be able to perform. We want them to learn skills like outlining, multiplying and researching. These are terms which, under specifiable conditions, constitute skill objectives in terms by which we can measure our learners' performance.

We either teach our learners *what they want or need to be able to do* or we teach them *the skills* to do what they want or need to be able to do. Thus, if we are not teaching a skill on a given day, then we teach the skills our learners will need in order to do whatever it is we are asking of them.

Asking The "Do" Questions

The basic question in developing the skill objective is: *who* is going to *do what* and at *what level?* A skill objective for the teacher, with regard to our content development skills, is that the *teachers develop their specialty contents* at the *skill level.*

We may attempt to develop the skill objectives in our specialty contents. The skill objective will always involve an action or behavior and, thus, an action word or verb. For example, if we are teaching our learners to supply the missing verbs in a sentence, then we may state our skill objective as: given a list of verbs, the *learners will supply a correct missing verb in eight out of ten* sentences. Or, if we are teaching our learners how to order numbers in the study of place values in mathematics, then we may state our skill objective as: our *learners will state "greater than" relationships among numbers between zero and ninety-nine.* If we are teaching learning skills in a Social Studies curriculum, we may state our first skill objective as follows: the *learners* will learn to *attend physically* to the learning experience at the *highest level* of attentiveness.

Skill Objective: The learners will learn to attend physically to the learning experience (teacher and materials) at the highest level of attentiveness (posturing and eye contact).

Asking The "Think" Questions

We can further refine our skill objectives by answering other basic questions. These questions define the conditions of the achievement of the skill objectives. They involve the things we must think about before we begin writing our skill steps.

These questions are most easily asked in the form of the basic interrogatives or 5 W's:

WHO? Who is involved?
WHAT? What is involved?
WHERE? Where should it be done?
WHEN? When should it be done?
WHY? Why is this skill important?

The answers to these "think" questions will further define the operations of the skill objective. They will also become the things the learners will need to learn about the skill objective.

Answering the Basic Interrogatives

The conditions of the skill objective, then, are defined by the answers to the basic interrogatives. For example, if we are teaching attending physically as our learning skill objective, we might answer the think questions as follows:

Skill Objective: The learners will learn to attend physically to the learning experience (teacher and materials) at the highest level of attentiveness (posturing and eye contact).

WHO? the learners
WHAT? learning materials
WHERE? classroom
WHEN? school day
WHY? preparation for learning

The definition of these conditions makes the skill objective achievable and functional.

Developing Skill Objectives

Try to develop the skill objective in your specialty content. First, answer the question: *"Who will do what at what level?"*

Remember to use a verb to define the action. Also, define the level of achievement in accordance with your knowledge of the specialty content.

Second, answer the *think* questions in your specialty content. The answers will help to further define the operations of the skill objective.

Skill Objective: _____

WHO? _____

WHAT? _____

WHERE? _____

WHEN? _____

WHY? _____

Defining The Learning Objective

Clearly, it is not enough to define the skill objective. Many people think that when they have defined a performance, behavioral, management or skill objective, that they have achieved it. This is not the case. To define what we need to do is not the same as doing it. But it is the first step toward achieving our goal.

Defining the skill objective, then, is the beginning of a very exciting adventure. We are taking people somewhere that they have not been before. It is just as exciting as defining the lunar-orbit rendezvous to put a person on the moon, or describing the growth of a child here on earth.

It is just as scary, too! For defining the skill objective is merely the first step. If we do not develop and implement all of the steps we need to achieve our skill objective, we will fail.

DEVELOPING SKILL STEPS

Achieving Goals with Steps

Not everything about achieving the skill objective is an exciting adventure. Once we have decided upon our skill objective, we must develop the skill steps to achieve that objective. The skill steps, to be sure, flow from the skill objective. They constitute the often complex follow-through program that enables us to achieve our learning objective.

For example, having defined the objective of putting a person on the moon, NASA became involved in the long and arduous process of developing the mechanical steps needed in order to accomplish the lunar-landing operations. This otherwise painful process was made joyful by the sense of accomplishment that accompanied the achievement of each sub-objective.

Skill steps, then, are the mechanical details we implement on our way to the skill objective. They are often sheer drudgery. They are the price we must pay to achieve our goals. They are the demands which we make upon ourselves that test our commitments. In the words of one teacher, "The skill steps are a journey through hell on our way to our heavenly objectives."

Atomizing the Skill Performance

We develop our skill steps by listing the steps the learners will follow to perform the skill. The first step tells the learners where to begin. The final step concludes in the skill objective. The intermediary steps contain all the instructions which the learners need in order to do the skill correctly.

In developing skill steps, we must realize that there are many things that are automatic for us that are not automatic for the learners. We have performed the skill so many times that we have mastered it. It is critical that we make all of the steps involved explicit in order to insure the learners' achievement of the skill objective.

Each step should reflect the learners' abilities to perform. In other words, it should be a step that all learners can perform successfully. For example, if we want the learners to supply the missing verb in a sentence, then the first step might be to read the sentence. If we want the learners to state "greater than" relationships in ordering numbers, the first step might be to draw a number line including the two numbers being compared. The succeeding steps are as atomistic as you can make them.

Content Development

Levels
> **Skill Steps** The steps we take to perform the skill objective.
>
> **Skill Objective** What we want or need to be able to do.

Asking The "How" Question

The basic question in developing the skill steps is *how* the learners will accomplish the skill objectives. The first "how" question asks: "*How* do the learners do the skill?"

For example, in terms of content development skills, *how* do the teachers develop their content? The answer to this question requires knowledge of the specialty content area, in this instance content development skills. It involves the development of the facts, concepts, principles, skill objectives and skill steps required to achieve the skill to be learned. It began with the first step of identifying the skill objective: What do we want our learners to be able to do?

If we are teaching attending physically as our learning skill objective, we might answer the "how" question as follows:

> **Skill Objective:** The learners will learn to attend physically to the learning experience (teacher and materials) at the highest level of attentiveness (posturing and eye contact).
>
> **HOW:** 1. Square with the teacher and/or learning materials
> 2. Lean toward the teacher and/or learning materials
> 3. Make eye contact with the teacher and/or learning materials

The answers to the "how" questions will yield our skill steps. But they are still incomplete.

Asking the "Check Step" Question

Just when we think that we have all of the skill steps, we find that there is still another question about how the skill is to be performed. We may think of this question as the *check step*. It asks:

"How will the learners know whether they are performing or have performed the skill steps correctly? How can they evaluate their own work? How can they become independent?"

For example, with regard to content development skills, how will teachers know whether they have developed their content correctly? The ultimate answer to this *check step* involves whether the learners have all the steps which they need to achieve the skill objective.

If we are teaching attending physically as our learning skills objective, we might answer the *check step* as follows:

> **Skill Objective:** The learners will learn to attend physically to the learning experience (teacher and materials) at the highest level of attentiveness (posturing and eye contact).
>
> **CHECK STEP:** 1. Facing the source of learning (right shoulder to left shoulder of person or left edge of materials)
> 2. Leaning forward or toward source at a twenty degree angle sitting, or a ten degree angle standing
> 3. Able to see the person or materials continuously

The answers to the *check step* will allow both the learners and teacher to measure the learners' performances using the same criteria.

Developing Skill Steps

Try to develop the skill steps in your specialty content. First, ask the "how" question: *How* will the learners do the skill? The answers will yield your skill steps.

Second, answer the *check step*: *How* will the learners know whether or not they have performed the steps correctly? The answers will yield additional skill steps to assess the learners' performance.

Skill Objective: _____

HOW?   1. _____

            2. _____

            3. _____

            4. _____

            5. _____

CHECK STEP: 1. _____

            2. _____

            3. _____

            4. _____

            5. _____

The answers to these questions will tell us whether we are ready to move on to our next step toward the skill objective.

Ensuring Goal Attainment

It is oftentimes quite frustrating to develop our content. We add step upon step in order to pay for our programmatic insurance policy, in hopes that no hole be left in our content lest one of our learners fall in.

Imagine if a step were left out of the lunar-orbit rendezvous program. No one would have walked on the moon. Or someone might have been stranded on the moon. If steps had been left out of the lunar-landing operations, there would definitely have been casualties.

In a similar manner, there will be casualties in learning – if we leave out steps in our careful construction of a human being. The key is what will be effective for our learners.

No step is too small! If a learner cannot perform a task, we must assume that we have not broken the task down into small enough steps. At the same time, we do not want to leave the human being out of the human equation. Teachers say that they do not want to become the "mechanical monsters" of content. They want to become "personalized people producers."

IDENTIFYING THE NECESSARY FACTUAL INFORMATION

Knowing What Things Are

Knowledge is a necessary but not sufficient condition of skill acquisition. Because we know *about* something does not mean that we can *do* it. But knowing about something can help us to do it. Knowing what things are involved can facilitate performing the skill steps.

For example, when NASA developed the spacecraft parts to accomplish the lunar-landing operations, they required a detailed labeling process. Without the ability to identify what things are, such a magnificent accomplishment could not have taken place.

Facts, then, are the labels that we attach to things in order to identify them. They are the names of people, places and things involved in the skill steps.

Naming Things

Indeed, it is interesting to think of facts as people. In that way, they live for us, and we will relate them to supporting the lifeful performance of skill steps.

If we did not know the names of people who we met, we would not be able to identify them other than by our senses. We could not recall them except by detailed descriptions. Further, we could not teach other people how to call for them or greet them or relate to them.

Facts, then, are nouns that identify things just as if they were people. They answer the questions: "What is it?" or "Who is it?" They enable us to work with the things that will facilitate our performance of skills in our lives.

Content Development

Levels
Skill Steps: The steps we take to perform the skill objective.
Skill Objective: What we want or need to be able to do
Facts: The names of the people, places and things involved in the skill steps.

Labeling People, Places & Things

It should be no problem for us to identify facts from our past experience. Facts are what we teachers spent most of our time studying during our own schooling. As learners, facts are the things we stayed up at night to memorize. Now, unfortunately, we have forgotten most of them.

As teachers, facts are what we review each day in our lesson plans in order to stay ahead of our learners. They are the things about which our prepared ditto tests and worksheets ask our learners. The final outcome –forgetfulness – will be the same for them as it was for us. Unless we can relate these facts to the performance of skills!

The very process in which we are now engaged is one of identifying facts. Labeling things as facts, concepts, principles, skill objectives or skill steps is a process of identifying facts. The facts that we teach our learners, are those related to the performance of the skills we teach them.

Supporting Skills with Facts

Facts, then, take on significance in relation to skills. They name the parts or components of the skills. They are the things which are directly involved when we take the steps to perform the skill.

To relate our facts to skill performance we need to ask ourselves: "Do my learners need to know this fact to do this skill?" and "Will knowing this fact help my learners to do this skill better?" Teaching the supportive facts will help us to keep our content relevant.

For example, we may identify certain facts in teaching our learners how to learn. In teaching attending physically as our skill objective our learners must know what *eye contact* is before they can make eye contact with their teachers or their learning materials. Indeed, they must know what *learning materials* are before they can posture themselves in relation to the materials. (Keep in mind that we need only to identify the facts that would present your learners with difficulty – not *every* fact.)

Skill Objective:	The learners will learn to attend physically to the learning experience (teacher and materials) at the highest level of attentiveness (posturing and eye contact).
Skill Steps:	1. Square with the teacher and/or learning materials
	Facts: teacher, learning materials
	2. Lean toward the teacher and/or learning materials
	Facts: none (learners already know the "teacher")
	3. Make eye contact with the teacher and/or learning materials
	Facts: eye contact

Identifying Factual Information

We can develop the facts in any specialty content. For example, in mathematics, in stating "greater than" relationships when ordering numbers we may develop the following steps and supportive facts:

Skill Objective:	The learners will learn to state "greater than" relationships
Skill Steps:	1. Draw number line to include the two numbers being compared
	Facts: number line, numbers
	2. Find number farthest to the right
	Facts: none
	3. Write the greater number, then "<" symbol and finally the number to the left on the number line
	Facts: symbol: ">"
	4. Read what you have written to yourself
	Facts: none

Developing Facts From Skill Steps

In a similar manner, we can determine the supportive facts that our learners must know in order to do the skill steps. Simply ask whether the learners need to know the facts before they can do the skill steps. Include only the names of people, places or things that are involved in performing the skill steps.

Skill Objective: _____

Skill Steps: 1. _____

                Fact: _____

            2. _____

                Fact: _____

            3. _____

                Fact: _____

            4. _____

                Fact: _____

            5. _____

                Fact: _____

Learning Useful Facts

Now we have the facts we need to support the learning of our skill steps. We have the first level of knowledge about the skills we intend to conquer. We are able to label the parts or components in order to identify them.

Developing the facts is part of the follow-through process in pursuing our skill objective. No longer do memorizing and regurgitating names and dates and places have the functional autonomy they once had. Now the learning of facts can be related to the achievement of skill objectives.

Clearly, it is not enough to identify the components in a skill step. We must also identify "what they do" and "how and why they do this" in order to complete our supportive knowledge base.

IDENTIFYING CONCEPTS

Attaching Meaning to Things

Perhaps the most exciting level of content involves the development of concepts. Often, long before we define our skill objective and initiate the process of developing content, we have concepts of what things mean and what they do. When we attach meaning to something, then we have begun to form a concept.

There are no boundaries to our concepts at this stage of our thinking. We can conceive of our wildest fantasies – like putting a person on the moon – or making our teaching classes effective here on earth. This is the fun stage of exploration. It is like the students' fantasies of achievement before the school year begins. Or the teacher's resolutions after a rehabilitative summer vacation. Or NASA's "think tank" operations before the President said, "Put a person up there!"

There is another stage of conceptual development. It follows the operational definition of the skill objective and skill steps. It elaborates upon the supportive factual knowledge that we have developed. It describes what we know about something.

For example, when NASA became involved in assigning spacecraft parts to accomplish the precise functions of certain objectives, it was involved in objectifying the concepts of the functions of the lunar-landing operation. In other words, it not only described the components, but it also defined what they do or what part they play, in a particular step in the operation. Each function provided on a small scale the same excitement that was accomplished by the final mission.

Describing Facts

What we know about a fact is called a concept. Concepts describe the nature or characteristics of things. They answer the question, "What is known about the fact?"

45

Conceptual learning enables us to organize what we know. We can name what we know. We can describe one or more aspects of the thing that we know.

Concepts are easy to identify. They are what most of us communicate in our conversations. Our concept of "sitting" enables us to recognize the object we sit on as a chair, even if it doesn't have legs. A child's concept of "hot" may be identical to the object, or fact – "stove." Later, the child may attach additional facts and concepts to the word, "hot" such as "match," "friction" and "molecular motion," as his or her concept of hotness expands.

Content Development

Levels:
    Skill Steps: The steps we take to perform the skill objective.
    Skill Objective: What we want or need to be able to do.
    Concepts: Tell something about a fact.
    Facts: The names of the people, places and things involved in the skill steps.

Identifying Concepts

In practice, concepts are what remain after we have identified nouns as facts. Concepts include all of the verbs, adverbs and adjectives that tell us about our facts.

The process in which we are engaged involves many concepts. Defining what skill objectives, skill steps, facts, concepts and principles do involves developing concepts. For example, the following definitions involve concepts:

Facts *label what things are.*

Concepts *identify what things do and what they mean.*

Principles *describe why they are important and when and where to use the skill objective.*

Skill objectives *define what we need to be able to do.*

Skill steps *detail how to perform the skill objective.*

Determining The Necessary Concepts

Like facts, then, concepts take on significance in relation to skills. To relate concepts to skill performance we need only ask: "Do my learners need to know the concepts to do the skill?"

For example, in teaching attending physically as your skill objective, it is necessary for the learners to understand certain concepts before they can implement any skill steps. Before the learners can square and posture themselves in relation to the teacher or the materials, they must understand the concepts of squaring and posturing. Before the learners can lean forward, they must understand the concepts of leaning and forward. (As in the identification of facts, only bother to identify the concepts that would present a problem for your learners.)

Skill Objective: The learners will learn to attend physically to the learning experience (teacher and materials) at the highest level of attentiveness (posturing and eye contact).

Skill Steps: 1. Square with the teacher and/or learning materials
    Concepts: Posture, square
    Facts: teacher, learning materials
2. Lean toward the teacher and/or learning materials
    Concepts: Lean, toward
    Facts: none (learners already know the "teacher")
3. Make eye contact with the teacher and/or learning materials
    Concepts: None
    Facts: eye contact

Identifying The Concepts in Each Step

We can develop the supportive concepts in any specialty content. For example, in mathematics, when stating "greater than" relationships in ordering numbers we may develop the following supportive concepts:

Skill Objective: The learners will learn to state "greater than" relationships

Skill Steps: 1. Draw number line to include the two numbers being compared
    Concepts: draw, compare
2. Find number farthest to right
    Concepts: find, farthest, right

3. Write the greater number, then ">" symbol and finally number to the left on the number line
    Concepts: write, left, greater, smaller
4. Read what you have written to yourself
    Concepts: none (learner already understands the term "read")

Developing Sample Concepts

In a similar manner, we can determine the supportive concepts that are necessary for our learners to know to do the skill steps. Simply ask whether the learners need to know the concepts to do the skill steps. To check our discriminations, we may ask ourselves if the concepts we have selected are verbs, adverbs or adjectives.

Skill Objective: _____

Skill Steps: 1. _____

Concepts: _____

2. _____

Concepts: _____

3. _____

Concepts: _____

4. _____

Concepts: _____

5. _____

Concepts: _____

Supporting Skills With Concepts

Now we have the facts and concepts that we need in order to

support the learning of our skill steps. We have the first two levels of knowledge about the skills we need to conquer. We are able to identify the parts and their functions in the implementation of the skill steps.

Again, developing the concepts is part of the follow-through on our commitment to achieve our skill objective. Concepts allow us to enter the future with our dreams – even our fantasies. They also help us to develop the functional knowledge to support the operations of the objectives into which we have translated our concepts.

Now we must complete our final level of knowledge. We know what things are and what they do. Now we must identify why they are important and where we use them, in order to complete our supportive knowledge.

DEVELOPING PRINCIPLES

Principles Are Relationships

The level of conceptual development that is most uniquely human is the level of principles. Principles organize our facts and concepts and relate one stable body of knowledge to another. They enable us to interpret our worlds and to deduce testable hypotheses based upon these interpretations. In this manner, principles not only account for past relationships, but also allow us to find new relationships.

For example, the entire lunar-landing operation was based upon the principles of physical science. One set of phenomena was functionally related to another. All phenomena were related to the total space mission of putting a person on the moon. Without the functional relationships described by scientific principles, the entire space phenomenon could not have taken place.

Principles, then, are often "cause-and effect" relationships that exist between phenomena. They are our theoretical notions of how and why something is taking place. They give us a sense of intellectual power over our universe, a power that we must ultimately test through our experience.

Why, When & Where of Content

There are many principles related to every skill we teach. The most important kind of principles describe why something works the way it does and why it is important. These principles help learners to understand how their world works. They answer the learners' question, "Why?"

"When the big hand goes around one time, one hour has passed."

"If you use a ruler to steady the pencil, the line will be straight."

"If you increase the angle of an inclined plane, then the effort needed to push the block will also increase."

Each of these principles deals with the idea of "cause-and-effect." They explain a cause-and-effect relationship for some aspect of a skill.

Content Development

Levels:

Skill Steps:	The steps we take to perform the skill objective.
Skill Objective:	What we want or need to be able to do.
Principles:	Why it works that way, why it is important, when or where to use the skill objective.
Concepts:	Tell something about a fact.
Facts:	The names of the people, places and things involved in the skill steps.

Cause-And-Effect Relationships

Principles are more difficult to identify than facts and concepts. One way to identify principles is to determine whether a particular phenomenon can fit the following format:

"If _____ , then _____ ."   A principle can usually be phrased in an "If _____ , then _____ " statement. Following the "if" is the cause. Following the "then" is the effect.

For example, in teaching writing, we can develop the following principles:

"If you outline your paper before writing it, then your ideas will build upon each other."

"If you write a topic sentence for your paragraph, then you'll be identifying the main idea of the paragraph."

The "if" is the skill step we are teaching our learners, while the "then" is the skill itself. Our learners can now understand how the skill step works.

Learner Benefits

This cause-and-effect principle can be extended to describe why something is important to our learners. We can do this by employing the following format:

"If _____ , then _____ , so that _____ ."

This principle hooks up the content with the learners' frames of reference. The principle does this by answering the question, "How will the learners benefit from this skill?"

"If you outline your paper before writing it, then your ideas will build upon each other, so that you won't be at a loss for what to write next."

"If you write a topic sentence for your paragraph, then you'll be identifying the main idea of the paragraph, so that your additional sentences will relate to the topic sentence."

In this manner, we can identify the skills and the benefits for the learners: "If (skill steps), then (skill objective), so that (learner benefits)." Doing the skill becomes the "cause" and the learner benefits become the "effect."

Principles and Supportive Knowledge

Like facts and concepts, then, principles take on significance in relation to skills. To relate our principles to skill performance we need only ask: "Do my learners need to know the principles to do the skill?"

For example, if attending physically is your skill objective, we can develop the following principle: "If you square, lean forward and make eye contact, then you will attend physically so that you will know you are ready to see and hear the teacher and the learning materials."

The statement of the principle incorporates the skill steps in accomplishing the skill objective and the learner benefits. It also incorporates the facts and concepts supporting the performance of the skill steps.

Skill Objective: The learner will learn to attend physically to the learning experience (teacher and materials) at the highest level of attentiveness (posturing and eye contact).

Principle: If the learners square, lean forward and
(Incorporates make eye contact, then they will attend
skill steps, facts physically, so that they will know that they
and concepts) are ready to see and hear the teacher and the learning materials.

"If _____ Then _____" Statements

We can develop the supportive principles in any specialty content. For example, in mathematics, when stating "greater than" relationships in ordering numbers we may develop the following supportive principle:

Skill Objective: The learners will learn to state "greater than" relationships.

Principle: If the learners put the larger number first and the smaller second, then they will be stating a "greater than" relationship so that they can put numbers in order of size.

In a similar manner, we can determine the supportive principles that are necessary for our learners to know in order to do the skill steps. Simply ask whether the learners need to know the principle to do the skill steps. Use the format: "If [skill steps], then [skill objective] so that [learner benefit]." In this manner, we will link the skill objective and skill steps to the learners and thus personalize the learning.

Skill Objective: _____

Principle: _____

Principles Relate Content To Learners

Now we have the facts, concepts and principles which we need to support the learning of our skill steps. We have all of the levels of knowledge which we need to conquer. We are able to identify the parts, functions and reasons for the implementation of the skill steps.

Again, developing the principles is part of the follow-through on our commitment to achieve our skill objective. Principles allow us to relate our facts and concepts to our skill steps; our skill steps to our skill objective; our skill objective to learner benefits.

In short, principles empower us to relate our current learnings to our future potential. Ultimately, they are our link with creativity.

SUMMARIZING THE CONTENT

Our expertise in our content is what makes us teachers. We do not have anything to offer if we do not have a specialty content. Preparing content means developing it in a form that makes it achievable for learners. Developing content involves programmatically developing the levels of conceptual development.

Before we move on to learning to deliver our content, let us take stock of how far we have come. Remember, initially you asked yourselves what it is you wish to share with your learners. Or, put another way, you asked what the most important dimensions of your content are. Address these questions again:

_____

_____

_____

_____

_____

Perhaps you can again take some aspect of your specialty content and outline how you would now develop the dimensions you have just noted in order to maximize student learning. This will give you an index of how well you have learned your content development skills.

_____

_____

_____

_____

_____

The Components of The Model

First, we can define the skill objective by answering the basic "do" question: *who* is going to do *what* and at *what* level? We can further refine this skill objective by answering the basic "think" questions: *who?*, *what?*, *where?*, *when?*, *why?*.

Second, we can develop the skill steps by answering the basic "how" question: *how* will the learners do the skill? In addition, we can check ourselves by answering the check step: how *will* the learners know that they are performing the skill correctly?

Third, we can develop the supportive knowledge for the skill steps by answering the basic knowledge questions:

Facts:	The names of the people, places and things involved in the skill steps.
Concepts:	Tell something about the facts.

Principles: Why it works that way, why it is important, when or where to use the skill objective.

If you have incorporated all of these steps in the development of your content, then you have achieved your own personal skill objective of applying your content development skills. If you have implemented the content development skills in your specialty content outlines, then you can develop your content for your learners.

Content Development

Levels:			
Skills:		**Skill Steps:**	The steps we take to perform the skill objective.
		Skill Objective:	What we want or need to be able to do.
Knowledge:		**Principles:**	Why it works that way, why it is important, when or where to use the skill objective.
		Concepts:	Tell something about a fact.
		Facts:	The names of the people, places and things involved in the skill steps.

Competence and Attitudes

Thus far, we have neglected our original concern with the positive learning attitude toward the content that we hope, along with skills and knowledge, to develop in our learners. This learning attitude is a product or, rather, a by-product of skills and knowledge development. The learners' positive learning attitude is defined by a growing feeling of competency and confidence in their skills and knowledge. Learning attitude has to do with their increasing abilities to manage themselves and their worlds.

The initial purpose of our positive learning attitude is to describe our worlds. The transitional purpose is to predict our worlds. The ultimate purpose is to control our worlds. Indeed, the ultimate goal of humanity is to control its destiny to the highest degree that it can.

About Achieving Goals

Having specialty contents to offer to other human beings is what makes us unique. The concern for developing and transmitting skills and knowledge is what separates human beings from other forms of life. Although other animals model limited skill learning after older animals, they do not utilize the didactic sources of learning we are about to address. This is available only to humans.

In addition, developing our specialty contents is what enables us as human beings to reach with our intellects beyond the experiences we have already had. The development and convergence of different specialty contents makes movement from the known to the unknown possible for us.

With content development skills, any goal can be operationalized. And any goal that can be operationalized can be achieved with the implementation of skill steps and the support of knowledge.

Humankind's goals in space or on Earth are limited only by the boundaries of our intellect. Hopefully, we will not forego our home on Earth prematurely. Hopefully, we will reach for the stars here on Earth.

RESEARCH BACKGROUND: CONTENT DEVELOPMENT

Operationalizing Goals

The effectiveness of any area of human endeavor is contingent upon the ability to operationalize its goals. This principle holds not only in business and industry, which are concerned with the production of goods and services, but in all areas of human services: child welfare and development; adolescent and delinquency treatment; mental health; mental retardation; corrections; health care and geriatric treatment.

By operationalizing the goal, we break it down into the operations needed to achieve it. In other words, we break out the step-by-step procedures for accomplishing the goal. In short, by operationalizing the goal we make it achievable.

This principle holds for education. We determine the skills, knowledge and attitudes that we want our learners to have. We operationalize these teaching goals in observable and measurable terms. The basic principle of content is that all effective content culminates in a skill objective.

Integrating Skills and Supportive Knowledge

Historically, arguments have stated that skills and knowledge do not necessarily follow from each other. Ryle (1949) referred to the distinction between being able to state factual propositions, or "knowing that," and being able to perform the operations of the skill, or "knowing how." Facts and concepts do not necessarily produce skills unless teachers learn to translate them into skills. Similarly, skills-building does not necessarily incorporate the necessary supportive knowledge unless teachers are trained to do so.

A number of studies have indicated that widespread student outcomes can be achieved by structuring the content for analysis. The teacher's structuring and the students' use of cognitive functions have proved particularly effective for the acquisition and retention of knowledge, acquisition and application of tool skills and the resulting improvement of learner attitudes (Bruner, 1966; Lindvall and Bolvin, 1966; Tyler, 1966).

In general, teachers are most effective in developing their content when they select content objectives that are congruent with the needs of the learners (Aspy and Roebuck, 1977; Flanders, 1970). In this context, they develop their content by achieving the following objectives: specifying the content objectives with clarity in terms of the learners' terminal skill behaviors (French, et al, 1957; Kearney, 1953; Mager, 1962); breaking down the content into the smallest possible skill steps and, presenting them to the learners (Lumsdaine, 1964; Smith and Moore, 1962); delivering the knowledge required to support the learning of the skill steps (Kaya, et al, 1967).

Developing A Functional Taxonomy

Perhaps the best known and most researched of instructional goals for content development is the taxonomy of educational objectives for the cognitive domain (Aspy and Roebuck, 1977; Bloom, et al, 1956; Metfessel, Michael and Kirsner, 1969). The cognitive domain deals with objectives related to the recall or recognition of knowledge, and the development and application of skills.

The taxonomy is divided into two major categories: skills and knowledge. These categories are further subdivided, with each skill built upon and assuming the acquisition of the previous skill and supportive knowledge (Payne, 1968).

The taxonomy has been characterized as an educational-logical-psychological classification system (Krathwohl, 1964). It is "educational" because the categories correspond to those which concern a teacher in developing curricula and learning experiences. It is "logical" because its categories are precisely defined and can be subdivided. It is "psychological" because it is consistent with thought in the psychological sciences, although it is not tied to any particular theory.

Summary of Research Findings

In summary, the content development skills presented (Chapter 2) are derived from the earlier taxonomies (Berenson, Berenson and Carkhuff, 1978). As such, they maximize the conditions of content development which facilitate student learning. The skill objectives facilitate the definition of learner terminal behaviors. The skill steps break the skill objectives down into atomistic and achievable learner steps. The development of facts, concepts and principles offers all of the supportive knowledge required for the learners to acquire the skill steps. Content development skills offer a comprehensive approach to developing content for student learning.

In conclusion, we cannot achieve any goals for human resource development or rehabilitation without systematically operationalizing these goals and programmatically operationalizing the steps to achieve them. In education, it is simply a matter of determining what we would like our learner products to look like, and developing our skills content to achieve these learning goals.

References

Aspy, D.N. and Roebuck, Flora N. *KIDS Don't Learn From People They Don't Like.* Amherst, Mass.: Human Resource Development Press, 1977.

Berenson, D. H., Berenson, Sarah R. and Carkhuff, R. R. *The Skills of Teaching – Content Development Skills.* Amherst, Mass.: Human Resource Development Press, 1978.

Bloom, B. S., Englehart, M. D., Furst, E. J., Hill, W. H. and Kratwohl, D. R. *A Taxonomy of Educational Objectives: Handbook I, The Cognitive Domain.* New York, N.Y.: Longmans, Green, 1956.

Bruner, J., ed. *Learning About Learning: A Conference Report.* Washington, D.C.: HEW, 1966.

Carkhuff, R. R. and Berenson, B. G. *Teaching As Treatment.* Amherst, Mass.: Human Resource Development Press, 1976.

Flanders, N. A. "Diagnosing and Utilizing Social Structures in Classroom Learning," in *The Dynamics of Instructional Groups*, National Society for the Study of Education, 59th Yearbook, Part II. Chicago, Ill.: University of Chicago Press, 1960.

Flanders, N. A. *Analyzing Teaching Behavior.* Reading, Mass.: Addison-Wesley, 1970.

Flanders, N. A. "Teaching Influence in the Classroom: Research on Classroom Climate," in *Theory and Research in Teaching*, A. Bellack, ed. New York, N.Y.: Columbia Teachers College, 1963.

French, W. and Associates. *Behavioral Goals of General Education in High School.* New York, N.Y.: Russell Sage Foundation, 1957.

Joyce, B. R. *Selected Learning Experiences.* Washington, D.C.: Association for Supervision and Curriculum Development, 1978.

Joyce, B. R. and Weil, M. *Models of Teaching.* Englewood Cliffs, N.J.: Prentice Hall, 1972.

Kaya, E., Gerhard, M., Stasiewski, A. and Berenson, D. H. *Developing a Theory of Educational Practice for the Elementary School.* Norwalk, Conn.: Ford Foundation Fund for the Improvement of Education, 1967.

Kearney, N. C. *Elementary School Objectives.* New York, N.Y.: Russell Sage Foundation, 1953.

Krathwohl, D. R. "The Taxonomy of Educational Objectives: Its Use in Curriculum Building," in *Defining Educational Objectives*, C.M. Lindvall, ed. Pittsburgh, Pa.: University of Pittsburgh Press, 1964.

Lindvall, C. M. and Bolvin, J. *The Project for Individually Prescribed Instruction.* Pittsburgh, Pa.: Learning Research and Development Center, University of Pittsburgh, 1966.

Lumsdaine, A. A. "Educational Technology, Programmed Learning and Instructional Science," in *Theories of Learning and Instruction*, National Society for the Study of Education, 63rd Yearbook, Part I. Chicago, Ill.: University of Chicago Press, 1964.

Mager, R. F. *Preparing Instructional Objectives.* San Francisco, Calif.: Fearon Publishers, 1962.

Metfessel, N. S., Michael, W. B. and Kirsner, D. A. "Instrumentation of Bloom and Krathwohl's Taxonomies for Writing of Educational Objectives." *Psychology in the Schools* 7: 227-231.

Payne, D. A. *The Specification and Measurement of Learning Outcomes.* Waltham, Mass.: Blaisdell, 1968.

Pfeiffer, I. L. "Teaching Inability – Grouped English Classes: A Study of Verbal Interaction and Cognitive Goals". *Journal of Teacher Education* 17: No. 3.

Ryle, Gilbert. *Concept of Mind.* New York, N.Y.: Barnes & Noble, 1949.

Smith, W. I. and Moore, J. W. "Size of Step and Curing." *Psychological Reports* 10:287-294.

Tyler, R. W. "New Dimensions in Curriculum Development." *Phi Delta Kappan* 48:25-28.

Lesson Planning Skills   3

DEVELOPING EFFECTIVE LESSON PLANS

Plans You Have Known

We apply many of the skills we learned in school without ever thinking about it. Reading newspapers and contracts are two illustrations. Making minor mathematical calculations to pay our bills or make out our income taxes are others. These are the basic tools of daily existence. They enable us to solve problems and achieve goals. Without them, we would be reduced to a more barren existence, immobilized by the demands of a highly technological society.

Unhappily, we are unable to do many other things. We do not even know what they are because we do not have the skills to implement them. We have totally forgotten the course work involving these skills, so we cannot even make the discrimination about what is possible.

The Principle of Effective Planning

We are frustrated because we cannot do many things that we should be prepared to do. We cannot handle many situations in our daily lives because we have forgotten the required skills.

Why do we lack so many skills? It is not just trigonometry or organic chemistry and the more esoteric courses that we have forgotten. It is actually most of the basic course work in most of the basic areas.

We have forgotten these skills because we never learned them in the first place. We never learned them because our teachers did not plan around skills application.

Planning, then, involves determining the application to which the skills will be put and developing a programmatic plan to achieve the ability to do this successfully. In other words, planning begins and ends with the skill application. In that context, the fundamental principle of lesson planning is this: *all effective lessons are organized around a skill application.* This is the topic of the following chapter.

Content Organization As Planning

Our teaching delivery is to our teaching preparation as marketing is to product development in business and industry. We have developed our product (our content). We now plan by organizing our content for marketing (lesson planning).

Planning for our marketing campaign does not have to be a dreary undertaking. It is every bit as exciting as planning for a ball game or a theatrical presentation. We must also plan for our teaching with the same care and detail.

In order to deliver the teaching product, then, we must first plan for it. We plan by organizing its content for delivery. We also plan by developing its methods of delivery.

Finally, we make the delivery of our content. We do this by using our plan. We implement the plan in conjunction with our interpersonal skills.

We are very fortunate in our marketing effort. We believe in our product. The challenge of marketing is to deliver the product in such a way that other people will come to believe in it too.

An Index of Your Planning Skills

As teachers, we have all had a lot of experience with lesson planning skills. Lesson plans are those notes we prepare before each school week begins. Using our textbooks and curricula, we write out what we will teach and how we will organize and teach it.

Before you learn content organizing skills, ask yourself the essential question about organizing your lesson: "How do I wish to organize this lesson?" Or, put another way, "What are the effective ingredients of organizing this lesson?" What do I call these content organization skills and what do they do? What are the principles that govern their effectiveness? How can they be defined as skills? How can I break out the skill steps to achieve these skills?

Skill Steps:
Skill Objective:
Principle:
Concept:
Facts:

At this point, it may be helpful for you to get an index of your previous learning about content organizing skills. Perhaps you can take a skill in your specialty content and outline how you would organize it.

_____

_____

_____

_____

_____

Effective Ingredients

If we seriously attempt to plan our lessons, there are many questions we should raise. These concern the effective ingredients of organizing our content.

Surely, the *presentation* itself is essential. This is the phase of our lesson where we present our skills and knowledge to our learners. Many of us believe this is all that is necessary. In practice, this is all many of us do.

But don't we also need some kind of a *review* of the learners' previous learning?

Would it also be helpful to develop some kind of an *overview* of the learning to be delivered?

What about *exercises* for the skills our learners have learned during the presentation?

Do we need a *summary* at the end of the learning experience? Further, can we define any or all of these lesson planning concepts as skill objectives and develop the skill steps to achieve them? Look at your outline of your specialty content and try to determine whether you have developed operational steps for implementing your lesson planning concepts. As we proceed through this chapter, keep in mind that, for now, you are only organizing the *content* of your lesson or teaching module. Later, you will make decisions about how this content is to be delivered.

The Content Organization System

We will quickly realize that we need all of these ingredients in combination. We want to insure our delivery to our learners. Most important, we want to insure the learners' reception of our content. To this end, we want to organize our content in an order that will facilitate the learners' reception of the content:

Reviewing the content to obtain a picture of the learners' abilities before learning.

Overviewing the content to share our images of the content with those of the learners.

Presenting the content to deliver our skills and knowledge to the learners.

Exercising the content to provide the learners with an opportunity to practice the skills.

Summarizing the content to obtain a follow-up picture of the learners' abilities after learning.

This is the *ROPES* framework of lesson planning skills learning which follows.

DEVELOPING AN EFFECTIVE REVIEW

Exploring Where The Learners Are

Before we teach our learners a new skill or learning objective, there are two things we must do. First, we should review what previous skills and knowledge our learners have. In other words, we are asking ourselves, "What other skills do our learners need to have before they can perform the new skill?" Second, we need to explore, "Where are our students coming from in terms of the new skill or learning objective?"

The answers to these questions give us an opportunity to get to know our learners. In particular, the review allows us to know where our learners are in relation to the content which we are about to deliver. Sometimes the review is a very illuminating teaching experience because we find out that our learners can perform many related skills and recall much supportive knowledge. Sometimes this is a very distressing experience, when we find out just how little they know and can perform.

At all times, we find that our learners' performances are reflections of how well they have been previously taught. After all, except for the beginning of a new course or unit or topic, we have taught them what they know and can perform in the review. The review gives us an opportunity to find out how well we have done our jobs. The review gives both teacher and learners the opportunity to explore where they are in relation to the content to be learned.

Checking Out The Contingency Skills

The review, then, gives us an opportunity to gauge the learners' levels of functioning on contingency skills, or skills that are required in order to perform the current skill. For example, in order to write a correct sentence, our learners must be able to write or print, spell and identify the subject and predicate, among other things. To multiply by a two-digit number, the learners need to have addition and regrouping skills.

The beginning of the lesson is the appropriate time to review the contingency skills which our learners have already learned. The skill we taught the previous day may be a contingency skill, or it may be so closely related to the new skill that we will want to review it. The learners may have learned the contingency skill last year, and we may want to determine how well they have retained it. In any event, before we begin to teach the new skill, we should review any contingency skills and any supportive knowledge required to perform these skills.

When we review, we are making a determination of where our learners are in relation to the new skill they are about to learn. The essential learning for the teacher at this point is, what can the learners already do, what do they already know, and how do they feel about the skill objective with which they are about to be presented?

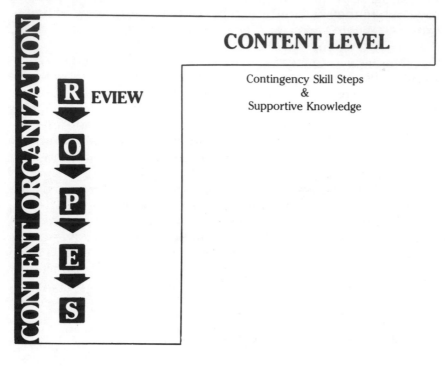

Diagnosing The Learners

The review, then, is a significant part of our lesson plan. We will use the review to diagnose where our learners are in relation to the content we are about to teach. In reviewing the contingency skills, in preparation for our first step toward the skill objective of attending physically, we may develop a review as our entry learning experience.

The teacher might use himself or herself, or the learners or any of a variety of other possibilities, as the source of the learning experience. For example, the teacher might ask the learners to describe and then show the ways that the teacher is attentive to the class. Or, perhaps more relevant, the teacher might have the learners freeze in their seats and take an index of their attending behavior in class before discussing it.

Review:

Tasks:

1. Freeze learners in seats.

2. Take index of learner postures.
3. Discuss learner postures.

Developing Review Tasks For the Lesson

The learners may be surprised by their postures. Just a moment before, they had thought they were attending to the learning experience. But were they really? Now, they are looking at the pictures of the postures they had assumed. Were they erect? Slouched? Slumped? Leaning forward? Sideways? Crooked? How much? How far? Did they make eye contact with the teacher or the materials? Continuously? Intermittently? Randomly?

Such review steps will yield an index of the learners' abilities to perform the skills involved, in this case, to attend physically to a learning experience. In addition, a discussion of the skill steps will yield an index of the level of supportive knowledge which the learners have about the skill.

At this point, list the learning tasks in which you would involve your learners when reviewing your content. Remember, the fundamental purpose of the review is to develop a learning experience which provides a diagnosis of the learners' levels of functioning in the skills and knowledge of your content. The nature of that learning experience can and should be as varied and creative as possible. At a minimum, it is an application which requires the students to demonstrate their readiness for the new learning.

Tasks:

Review: 1. _____

2. _____

3. _____

Reviewing – The First Step in Lesson Planning

The review, then, gives both teacher and learners an index of where the learners are functioning in relation to the content. This is precisely the function of the review: providing a situational diagnosis of where the learners are functioning upon entering the learning experience. The review is particularly critical if we implement the fundamental principle of learning: *all learning begins with the learner's frame of reference.*

The review gives us the opportunity to get to know our learners with intimacy. The intimacy is related to the content we are teaching. It helps us to avoid generalization and/or prejudice from previous learning experiences. It helps us to begin our learning journey with accurate knowledge of the starting point for each individual.

In summary, the learners enter the learning experience by exploring where they are in relation to it. The review gives us an index of the results of this exploration. The learners explore where they are in order to understand where they want or need to be with the learning tasks. That is the function of the overview.

FORMULATING AN EFFECTIVE OVERVIEW

Understanding Where Learners Want or Need To Be

Once we have a picture of where our learners are, we need to develop an overview of where they want or need to be. This is a very exciting part of content organization because now we get to share our teaching goals with the learners.

The overview can also be great fun because it gives our learners the opportunity to share their perspectives of the learning goals. The learners can also communicate their experiences of the skills to be learned.

The overview, then, provides both teacher and learners with an opportunity to share their images of the skills. By relating images, the learners can compare their experiences of the teaching goals with the teachers. At the same time, the teachers can compare their teaching goals with the learners' experiences of them. The net effect of this comparison of images is to facilitate the learners' understanding of where they are in relation to where they want or need to be.

Identifying Skill Applications

When we overview a new skill, we reach consensus with the

learners on a reason for learning the skill. The primary reason that we will use to motivate the learners will be skill applications or uses of the skill by the learners.

The skill applications and knowledge shared by the teacher will demonstrate the teacher's extensive repertoire of responses. The teacher can show competency on applications that are most relevant to learners: the teacher can do it better.

Thus, the math teacher may make the many rapid calculations required to figure out earned-run-averages in baseball or miles-per-gallon averages in driving in order to overview the learners toward multiplying instead of adding long columns of numbers before dividing. Or the English teacher may demonstrate an ability to write words, sentences and paragraphs or to draw posters, maps or charts in order to overview learning to print.

Then, instead of saying, "We know how to do that," the learners will say, "Teach us how to do that."

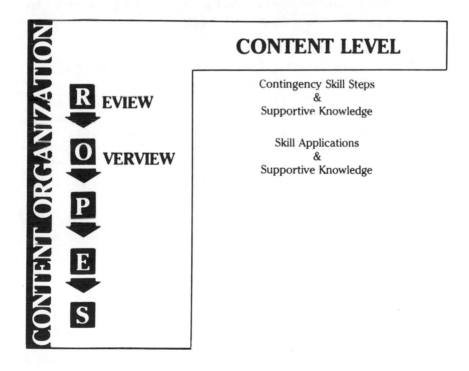

Setting Goals For The Learners

The overview, then, provides us with an opportunity to set goals for the learners. In the review, we diagnosed where the learners were in relation to the learning tasks. In the overview, we will set goals for where they want or need to be.

In overviewing the skill applications of attending physically, we can develop an overview of the skills to be learned. We will do this by developing the potential skill applications and relating them to the skills to be learned through the development of principles. Then we will develop a learning experience to incorporate the principles.

Overview: Skill Applications
Principles
1. If you learn to attend physically, then you can communicate attentiveness to others (your peers as well as adults).
2. If you learn to attend physically, then you can observe others (or learning experiences).
3. If you learn to attend physically, then you can listen to others (or learning experiences).

Experience
1. Place two learners back-to-back in chairs with the first one talking very quietly.
2. Rotate the other's chair slowly by degrees toward the first one.
3. Ask questions at each stage of rotation about the satisfaction of the above principles. (i.e., "Does this position communicate attentiveness?" "Can you see the other person?" "Can you hear the other person?"

Developing Overview Tasks For The Lesson

This overview can be a very dramatic illustration of a skill application. But it is also directly relevant to real-life skill applications. The learners will find that the more closely they attend physically, the more they are attentive, observing and listening. Conversely, any deviation from a fully attentive posture detracts from their level of attentiveness, observing and listening.

Such an overview will help the learners to understand not only where they are but where they want to be. The skill application in conjunction with the learning experience will make learning the skills desirable for the learners.

At this point, list the skill applications that will overview the skills for your learners. Remember to make the skill applications relevant to the learners' living more effectively in their worlds. Then, develop one or more learning experiences to demonstrate the skills applications.

Overview: Skill Applications
Principles

1. _____

2. _____

3. _____

Learning
Experience

Overviewing – The Second Step In Lesson Planning

The overview, then, gives both teachers and learners an opportunity to understand where the other is "coming from." Most important, it gives the learners a picture of where they are "going to." This is precisely the function of the overview: providing a cognitive map to guide the learners through their learning experiences.

The overview gives the learners an opportunity to be introduced to the content. Through the demonstration of skill applications, the learners can understand where they want to be with regard to the skills. It is an exciting moment for both teacher and learners, as they get a glimpse of future learning.

In summary, the review helps the learners to explore where they are by demonstrating their contingency skills. The teacher then helps the learners to understand where they want or need to be by overviewing the skill application. It now remains for the teacher to act, to get the learners from where they are to where they want to be. This is the function of the presentation.

PLANNING AN EFFECTIVE PRESENTATION

Getting The Learners To The Objective

After we have organized our review and overview of the content, we are ready to develop our presentation. When we present, we teach our learners how to perform the skill. The presentation is the "how to do it" part of organizing the content.

While the presentation is the most involved part of content organization, it also provides us with an opportunity to demonstrate our expertise. It is this expertise that makes us teachers. It is the moment of presentation that makes us most proud of our skills and knowledge in our content, and our ability to deliver it.

The presentation, then, provides us with an opportunity to deliver our content to our learners. It gives us a chance to initiate action steps that will get our learners from where they are, to where they want to be.

Breaking Down The Skill

In order to prepare our presentations, we must break down the skill steps our learners need to take in order to perform the skill. This is the most critical part of our planning. In effect, this means breaking down the skill into learner-sized steps. How many times have we heard our learners say:

"What do I do first?"

"What do we do next?"

What our learners are really asking for are the steps and knowledge they need to successfully perform the skill. What we must do is break down the skill into the steps the learners require.

For example, in teaching our learners to print something as simple as an "i", we might break the skill steps down as follows: (1) start pencil on middle line; (2) draw a straight line down; (3) stop at bottom line; and (4) dot over top. Or to print a "t," we might develop the following steps: (1) start on top line; (2) draw a straight line down; (3) stop at bottom line; and (4) make a horizontal line, stopping at the right of the vertical line.

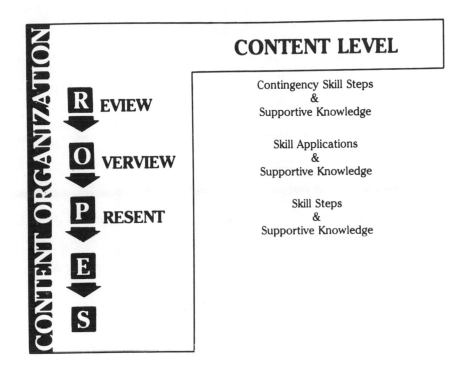

Developing Skill Steps

Breaking down a skill into skill steps is the critical core of organizing content. The steps tell our learners exactly what to do and in what order. If we write out the skill steps completely, then the learners can successfully perform them. If we can develop the steps together with our learners, then we will have involved them in their own teaching.

If the skill steps are incomplete, the chances are that the learners will be unsuccessful. If we leave out a step, then our learners will fall into the hole. One way of checking our steps is for us to actually perform what we have written.

For example, in presenting attending physically, we may break down the skills to include all the skill steps necessary for their performance. In order to do this, we must define our skill objective. We must also develop all of the supportive knowledge required to perform the skill steps. We will recognize that we have already developed our content for this purpose.

Presenting: Attending Physically

Skill Objective: The learners will learn to attend physically to the learning experience (teacher and materials) at the highest level attentiveness (posturing and eye contact).

Skill Steps: 1. Squaring with the teacher and/or learning materials.
2. Leaning toward the teacher and/or learning materials.
3. Making eye contact with the teacher and/or learning materials.

Supportive Knowledge:

Facts: teacher, learning materials, eye contact

Concepts: posture, squaring, lean, toward

Principle: If the learners square, lean forward and make eye contact, then they will attend physically so that they will know that they are ready to see and hear the teacher and the learning materials.

Devising Presentation Tasks For The Lesson

The learners should find all of the steps and knowledge in the presentation that they require to achieve the skill objective. In this regard, the steps should be so small or simple as to seem absurd. This atomistic simplicity will insure the learning.

The presentation, then, teaches the learners the skill steps they require to get from where they are to where they want to be with the skill. The performance of the skill steps enables the learners to perform the skill.

At this point, define the skill objective and list the skill steps. Also, indicate any supportive knowledge which is required in order to perform the skill steps. You should be able to draw from the content which you have developed to perform these tasks.

Presenting: Attending Physically
Skill Objective:
Skill Steps: 1. _____

2. _____

3. _____

Supportive Knowledge:
Facts: _____

Concepts: _____

Principles: _____

Presenting — The Third Step In Lesson Planning

The presentation, then, gives the teacher an opportunity to deliver to the learners the skill steps that the learners need. These skill steps, along with the supportive knowledge, will enable the learners to perform the skill. This is precisely the function of the presentation: to deliver the skills to the learners.

In turn, the presentation gives the learners an opportunity to get to know the content. The learners acquire skills and knowledge through the teacher's presentation. This is the heart of the learning experience for the learners. The presentation is a very intense moment. Exhilarating for the learners if effective, debilitating if not.

When appropriate, the teacher will (using some varying combination of methods) preview the entire skill for the learners. They will therefore come to know more accurately what the skill objective looks like. Then the teacher will walk the learners through the skill, step-by-step, to ensure that their first experiences with the skill are successful.

In summary, the review helps the learners to explore where they are with the skills. The overview helps them to understand where they want or need to be with the skills. Next, the presentation helps them to act to get from where they are to where they want to be with the skills. It now remains for the learners to have an opportunity to practice the skills, so that they can apply them when necessary. This is the function of exercising the skills.

PREPARING
AN EFFECTIVE
EXERCISE

Practicing The Skill Steps

The next part of our lesson plan is the exercise. The purpose of the exercise is simple: the learners need the opportunity to practice the new skill.

The learners have already been taught how to perform the steps of the skill during the presentation. They have had the opportunity to try the skills once. But once is not enough.

The exercise is really an opportunity for the learners to "own" the skill. By practicing it over and over, or by being exposed to individually prescribed learning experiences, they make it theirs and have it available for application as appropriate.

The exercise, then, facilitates the individual learners' receiving and incorporating the skills into their repertoires of responses. It serves to reinforce the action steps needed to get the learners from where they are to where they want to be.

Constructing Practice Exercises

The exercise of the lesson does not introduce any new content. Instead, it involves the learners in a repeated use of the new skill.

First, the skill will be performed by itself. Then the learners will do exercises which require them to use the new skill in conjunction with other skills.

The more times we can involve the learners in using the new skill, the more we increase their chances of being able to master it. A variety of practice materials and applications will keep the learning exciting.

Thus, for example, in a simple exercise for using printing skills, the teacher may use a variety of writing materials: pencil; pen; crayon; magic marker; paint; plain paper; lined paper; construction paper; newsprint.

In addition, the teacher may develop a variety of exercises around different skill applications incorporating other skills: writing words (spelling skills); writing sentences (writing skills); writing paragraphs (composition skills); or, drawing posters (measuring skills, drawing skills).

Varying The Practices

Practice makes perfect – provided the exercise involves skills. Introducing variety in the practice increases the probability of being perfect in making the skill application.

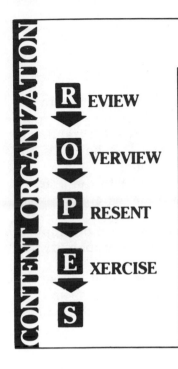

CONTENT LEVEL

Contingency Skill Steps
&
Supportive Knowledge

Skill Applications
&
Supportive Knowledge

Skill Steps
&
Supportive Knowledge

Skill Steps

We can introduce variety in both the materials and the applications. At all times, we will try to select experiences with which the learners will be successful. If the practice includes skills the learners have not learned, they will fail. In addition, we will always study the skill applications to determine what other skills the learners must use when they practice the new skill. We will select the applications which use the new skill in conjunction with other skills that the learners have already mastered.

For example, in developing practice exercises for attending physically, we may vary both the learning experiences (teachers and different materials) and the skills application (sitting and standing attending behavior). In addition, we can develop exercises which incorporate other skills (such as being prepared for class or preparedness skills).

Exercises: Attending Physically
1. While sitting, attend to the teacher.
2. While sitting, attend to learning materials (vary – books, chalkboard, audio materials, visual materials).
3. While standing, attend to teacher.

4. While standing, attend to learning materials (as above).
5. Repeat, with preparedness skills.

Designing Exercise Tasks For The Lesson

These exercises will give the learners a familiarity with the attending skills in a variety of different situations. The more variable the skill applications, the greater their generalizability or transferability. The more integrated they are with other skills, the more natural and useful will be their application.

The exercise, then, provides the learners with the practice which they require to get from where they are, to where they want to be with the skills. The exercise of the skill steps enables the learners to apply the skills in real life situations. The more applications we elicit from the learners, the greater is the probability that the learners will use the skill.

Now, develop exercises for practicing the skill steps. You should try to vary both the learning materials and the skill applications. Also, you will want to incorporate other skills that the learners have mastered, if appropriate.

Exercises: _____

1. _____

2. _____

3. _____

4. _____

5. _____

Exercising – The Fourth Step In Lesson Planning

The exercise, then, gives the learners an opportunity to practice the skills. Repetition with different materials and applications will increase the learners chances of making real life applications. This is precisely the function of the exercise: to practice the skills.

In turn, the exercise gives the learners an opportunity to get to know the content with intimacy. The learners repeat and apply the skills through their practice exercises. This is where learning is reinforced or extinguished. The exercises are the repetitive dry-runs which we make in preparation for the real thing.

In summary, the review facilitates learner exploration. The overview facilitates learner understanding. The presentation facilitates learner action through acquisition. Here, the exercises reinforce the learner action behavior by preparing for application. It remains for the learners to get an index of how well they have learned the skills and knowledge. This is the function of summarizing the skills.

PRODUCING AN EFFECTIVE SUMMARY

Checking Out What Has Been Learned

After we teach our learners the skills, we must summarize the learning. Here we are asking our learners, "What have you learned?"

The final part of our lesson, then, is our summary. The summary gives us another opportunity to assess where our learners are. Just as the initial review assessed the contingency skills, so does the summary assess the skills acquired by the learners during the learning experience.

Again, the results may be happy or sad. Happy if we have been effective in helping our learners to acquire the skill, sad if we have not been effective.

In this context, the summary is an index of our teaching. It provides both teacher and learners with an opportunity to explore where the learners are. It stimulates a recycling of the learning process of exploration, understanding and action.

Assessing Skill and Knowledge

What the summary really does is give us the opportunity to

review the new skill and knowledge with our learners. The learners may have forgotten a step. Or perhaps they never fully understood a part of what they were doing in the exercise.

We will take advantage of the summary to refocus our learners' attention on the steps of the skill. To do this, we will go back to the steps we developed for the presentation of the skill, then we will ask the learners to perform the skill once more.

Summarizing, then, serves the same function as reviewing. Where we reviewed the contingency skills to begin the organization of our content, we now use the skill steps from our presentation to summarize our content.

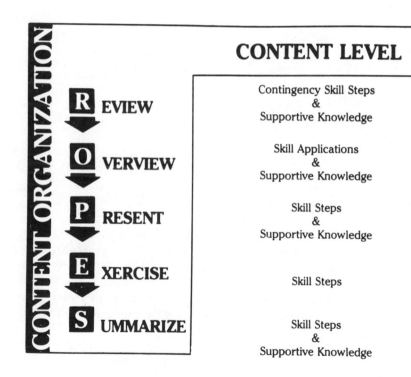

Diagnosing Competence

Just as the review did, then, the summary lets us diagnose where our learners are in relation to what we have taught. Most important, the summary provides the learners with the opportunity to diagnose themselves in relation to what they have learned.

Thus, the learners may summarize the steps of performing the skill. We, in turn, can diagnose where our learners are in relation to what we have taught. One way to develop the summary is to provide an experience, such as we initially did in the review. Our post-teaching assessment should resemble our pre-teaching assessment, so that we can get an index of the effects of our teaching. Having the learners develop their own summary experiences is a very acceptable alternative strategy.

Summary: **Tasks:**
1. Freeze learners in seat.
2. Have learners take index of learner postures.
3. Have learners discuss skill steps involved in learner postures.

Developing Summary Tasks For The Lesson

Hopefully, the learners will not be as surprised by their postures this time. They should know what the dimensions of attending physically are. They should be applying those dimensions in the classroom as well as in other experiences. They should be using these skills to observe, be attentive and listen to the sources of their learning.

Such summary steps will yield an index of what the learners have learned, in terms of both skills and knowledge. At this point, list the learning tasks in which you would involve our learners in summarizing the content. Remember, the fundamental purpose of the summary is to develop a learning experience which provides a diagnosis of the learners' levels of functioning in the skills and knowledge of your content.

Summary: **Tasks:**
1. _____

2. _____

3. _____

Summarizing – The Fifth Step In Lesson Planning

In a very real sense, the content is organized toward learner performance in the summary. That is to say, the summary provides the index of achievement of the skill objective, and the skill objective is the purpose of learning.

Just as with the review, then, the summary gives both teacher and learners an index of where the learners are functioning in relation to the content. And that is precisely the function of the summary: providing a situational diagnosis of where the learners are functioning upon exiting from the learning experience. The summary is particularly critical if we implement the fundamental principle of learning: all teaching culminates in achievement of the skill objective.

The summary gives us the opportunity to be honest with ourselves and our learners. It enables us to reinforce our effective teaching programs and to reshape our ineffective ones. It allows the learners to reinforce their effective learning efforts and to reshape their ineffective ones.

SUMMARIZING LESSON PLANNING SKILLS

Looking Over Your Planning Skills

Our expertise in planning and implementing lessons is what enables us to teach our skills. It is one thing to have expertise in content. It is another to be able to communicate that expertise, i.e., to teach it. Organizing the content is the first step in planning our teaching.

Before we move on to learning to develop our lesson plans fully, let us get an index of our content organization skills. Initially, you asked yourselves how you wished to organize your lesson. Or, put another way, you asked what were the effective ingredients of organizing your lesson. Now, address these questions again.

Outline any teaching methods and relevant supportive knowledge that you would employ in delivering our content. Use the teaching skills you have already learned. Use your content development skills to define your lesson planning skills.

Skill Steps: _____

Skill Objective: _____

Principle: _____

Concepts: _____

Facts: _____

Perhaps you can again take a skill from your specialty content and outline how you would organize it now. Use the teaching skills which you have already learned. Only this time, reproduce the teaching system involved. This will give you an index of how well you have learned your lesson planning skills.

_____

_____

_____

_____

_____

Reviewing The Planning Model

We can ask ourselves, again, about the effective ingredients of the organization of our content. Now we can respond with answers, rather than questions.

First, we can *review* the contingency skills and knowledge, in order to diagnose the learners;

Second, we can *overview* the skill applications and knowledge, in order to compare images and set learning goals;

Third, we can *present* the skill steps and knowledge, or develop the steps of our learning programs;

Fourth, we can *exercise* the skill steps and knowledge, or practice the skills;

Fifth, we can *summarize* the skill steps and knowledge, or diagnose the effects of teaching.

If we have incorporated all of these steps (ROPES) in the organization of our content, then we have achieved our own personal skill objective of applying our content organizing skills. If we can implement the specific lesson planning skills with our specialty content, then we can deliver our content to our learners.

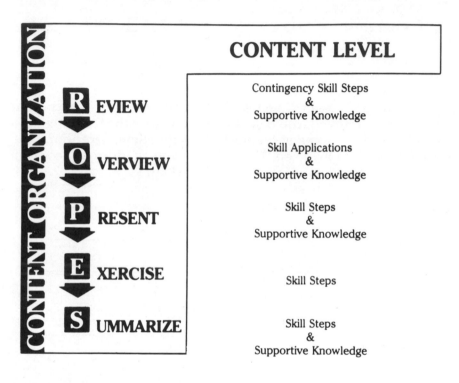

Planning For Human Learning

Seen together, the phases of organizing our content directly parallel our learners' involvement in learning.

Reviewing the content will give both the teacher and learners an opportunity to *explore* where the learners are in relation to the learning tasks.

Overviewing the content will allow both teacher and learners to *understand* where they are in relation to where they want to be with the learning tasks.

Presenting the content will enable the teacher to deliver the skills and knowledge to the learners so that the learners can *act* to accomplish their learning tasks.

Exercising the content will allow the learners to *act* to practice the skills they have acquired.

Summarizing the content will give both the teacher and learners an opportunity to *explore* again and recycle where the learners are in relation to the learning tasks.

Framing A Human Delivery

The *ROPES* order itself, then, is related to the *natural* movement of the learners through the learning process: exploring where they are; and understanding where they are in relation to where they want to be. Perhaps this is the most important contribution of content organizing skills: to facilitate the learners' cycling and recycling of the phases of learning.

In this respect, the *ROPES* organization is attuned to the most precious and fragile process of humankind: learning to become human through the transmission of the skills and knowledge which make us human. The teacher is a central factor in the transmission of these humanizing skills from one generation to the next. And the content of the lesson plan is organized to facilitate the transmission of these skills.

If our relationship to our content through our teaching preparation reflects our personal development, then our relationship to our learners through the organization of our content indicates the first stage of our own interpersonal development.

RESEARCH BACKGROUND: LESSON PLANNING

Lesson Organization

All content requires an organization that reflects its purpose. In other words, the content must be organized sequentially in order to achieve its purpose: making a skill application. Thus, means are necessary to assess the pre-instructional preparedness of the learners for the learning; to introduce the goals of the content; to present the mechanics of the content; to practice the skills, especially including applying them; and to summarize the post-instructional functioning of the learners.

Overall, the research indicates that teachers who organize their content in a way that is meaningful for the learners are most effective. Those teachers are most effective who review the contingency skills; overview the new skill applications; present, exercise and summarize the skill steps. Such a lesson plan provides the learners with maximum exposure to the skill steps leading sequentially to the application of the skills. The basic principle of content organization is that all effective lesson plans are organized around the skill application.

In the Program on Teaching Effectiveness·(1976), the teacher's "structuring" activities consisted of the following: reviewing the main idea and facets covered in the lesson; stating objectives at the beginning of a lesson; indicating important points in a lesson; summarizing the parts of the lesson as the lesson proceeded. All of these structuring functions were found to be related to teaching effectiveness and are incorporated in the ROPES lesson plan.

The Sources Of Effective Lesson Plans

The review is an opportunity for the learners to demonstrate their ability to perform the contingency skills and knowledge. In other words, the review has a diagnostic function. The learners cannot proceed to the new skill objective unless they can demonstrate their expertise in the old skill objective (Berenson, Berenson and Carkhuff, 1979).

The overview provides both teacher and learners with an opportunity to develop the skill application. That application is, after all, the purpose of the learning. In so developing, it is most helpful to relate the learners' images to the teachers' images. This provides for the possibility of bridging the gap between images (Berenson, 1977).

In presenting, teachers who present their skill steps in a responsive manner are most effective. That is, teachers who are open to input and feedback from the learners tend to modify their skill steps to meet learner needs. Thus, they use an indirect manner in influencing the learners to perform the skill steps (Flanders, 1965, 1966; Kaya, et al, 1967).

Giving learners additional time to exercise the skill steps results in anticipated increases in skills and knowledge. A circular relationship exists so that practicing with processes will lead to increased ability with processes. This principle is heavily supported by research (American Educational Research Association, 1966; McCullough, 1963). The data indicate quite specifically that, independent of the kinds of materials or methods used, increasing the time spent on learning tasks increases skill learning.

In terms of evaluating the learners in the summary, it is critical for teachers to test for the same skills and knowledge that they have taught. Thus, the summary becomes a post-test of the learning experience for which the original review was a pre-test.

Summary of Research Findings

In summary, lesson planning skills (Chapter 3) maximize the conditions that facilitate student learning (Berenson, Berenson and Carkhuff, 1978). The review facilitates the pre-learning diagnosis of contingency learner skill and knowledge needs. The overview provides the opportunity for examining skill applications. The presentation offers the skill steps needed to achieve the specified goals, in conjunction with the indirect influencing of the teacher, to facilitate the learners' achievement. The exercises provide opportunities for the learners to practice the skill steps. The summary provides the opportunity for a post-learning diagnosis of learner skills and knowledge. The content organizing skills offer a comprehensive approach to lesson planning for student learning.

In conclusion, the organization of the content reflects the essential purpose of the content: learning to make a skill application. All stages of organization must lead to and flow from this purpose. The purpose of all effective teaching is the effective learning of personally useful content.

References

American Educational Research Association. *Review of Educational Research.* Washington, D.C.: AERA, 1966.

Berenson, D. H. "The Teacher in the Learning Equation," in *Toward Excellence in Education*, R. R. Carkhuff and J. W. Becker, eds. Amherst, Mass.: Carkhuff Institute of Human Technology, 1977.

Berenson, D. H., Berenson, Sarah R. and Carkhuff, R. R. *The Skills of Teaching - Lesson Planning.* Amherst, Mass.: Human Resource Development Press, 1978.

Berenson, D. H., Berenson, Sarah R. and Carkhuff, R. R. *The Skills of Teaching - Teaching Delivery Skills.* Amherst, Mass.: Human Resource Development Press, 1979.

Flanders, N. A. *Teacher Influence, Pupil Attitudes and Achievement.* Washington, D.C.: HEW, 1965.

Flanders, N. A. *Interaction Analysis in the Classroom.* Ann Arbor, Michigan: School of Education, University of Michigan, 1966.

Kaya, E., Gerhard, M., Stasiewski, A. and Berenson, D. H. *Developing a Theory of Educational Practices for the Elementary School.* Norwalk, Conn.: Ford Foundation Fund for the Improvement of Education, 1967.

McCullough, C. M. "What Does Research Reveal About Practices in Teaching Reading?" in *Handbook of Research on Teaching*, N. L. Gage, ed. Chicago, Ill.: Rand McNally, 1963.

"Program on Teaching Effectiveness," *SCRDT.* Stanford, Calif.: Stanford Center for Research and Development in Teaching, 1976.

Teaching Methods Skills 4

DEVELOPING EFFECTIVE TEACHING METHODS

Experiences We Have Had With Methods

As learners, we have experienced many different kinds of teaching methods. Most often, in the early grades we had what we might call an "integrated" learning experience. Our early teachers used a variety of methods that told us about the content; they used a variety of methods to show us the content or how to use it; finally, they gave us an opportunity to do something with the content.

This was when we learned the most skills. Indeed, most of the skills that we rely upon in our daily living, learning and working activities were learned in elementary school, from teachers using a variety of teaching methods. Most important for our learning were those opportunities which we had to practice or do the skills involved. The more practice we have in using the skill, the more we retain an ability to use the skill in our daily lives. Indeed, the more varied our practice, the more we are able to make creative applications of what we learned.

The Principles of Effective Teaching Methods

Unfortunately, most of our learning experiences in our early education have not been "integrated." Consequently, we are frustrated, because there are many things that we know about but cannot do. This is because the level of teaching methods generally decreases as the level of "education" increases. Most significantly, all of those opportunities to do things, to build things, or to apply skills are gone. Concurrently, demonstrations of the skills and their applications by the teachers are also absent.

What is emphasized by teachers at secondary and post-secondary educational levels is largely didactic, largely telling about something rather than the doing of something. Thus, the learners learn how to talk about something, but they cannot do anything!

The missing step in secondary educational experience is the doing, or kinesthetic experience: the experience that allows us to file permanent images of the skill in our brains. Accordingly, the basic principle of teaching methods is this: *all effective teaching methods emphasize kinesthetic learning*. This is the topic of this chapter.

Variety And Effectiveness

There are as many different kinds of teaching as there are teachers. Some teachers emphasize the use of question-and-answer techniques. Others use a lot of programmed instruction. Still others utilize the overhead projector a great deal. In a very real sense, each teacher is a different teaching method. Indeed, each teacher feels "whole" when he or she is delivering the content using teaching methods. Probably more than anything else, the teaching methods reflect the uniqueness of the teacher.

Unfortunately, most teachers emphasize one teaching method to the exclusion of others. Many emphasize the didactic presentation, or lecture, most of the time. However, the really good teachers – the ones who not only keep us awake, but also involve us in learning – use a variety of teaching methods.

To be sure, there is a "variety principle" that characterizes effective teaching methods: the more methods the teacher employs the more effective is the teaching; the more different ways the teacher involves the learners, the more learning takes place. Thus the principle of variety carries with it the criterion of participation.

An Index Of Your Teaching Methods

A common problem is that many times we emphasize one or

the other teaching method without understanding its effectiveness as a source of learning. Often the methods we employ are randomly selected. Thus, the effects upon learning are randomly achieved.

Consider for a moment some of the teaching methods you employ. What are some of these teaching methods and what do they do? What are the principles that govern their effectiveness? How can they be defined as skills? How can we break out the skill steps to achieve the skills?

What Methods Do You Use to Teach Each Type of Content?

Skill Steps: ___ ___ ___ ___ ___

Skill Objective: ___ ___ ___ ___ ___

Principle: ___ ___ ___ ___ ___

Concept: ___ ___ ___ ___ ___

Facts: ___ ___ ___ ___ ___

At this point, it may be helpful to get an index of our previous learning about teaching methods. Perhaps you can take a skill in your specialty content and outline the methods you would employ to deliver it. In so doing, employ the content and teaching preparation skills you have learned.

Content Organization

Content Level (Identify)	R Contingency Skills	O Skill Applications	P Skill Steps	E Skill Steps	S Skill Steps
The Teaching Methods You Would Use To Deliver This Content	___	___	___	___	___
	___	___	___	___	___
	___	___	___	___	___
	___	___	___	___	___
	___	___	___	___	___

The Ingredients of Effective Teaching Methods

Clearly, there are many possible teaching methods we might list if we consider this area seriously.

Surely, the lecture or didactic presentation is familiar to all of us. The lecture is one of the methods which we use to *tell* our learners what to do and how to do it. The fact of delivering one person's content to another is supportive. The principle of the transmission of images through words is relevant to the lecture's effectiveness. Defining the skill objective and skill steps is more difficult. That is the topic of this lesson.

In addition, there are other concepts of teaching methods that we can develop. We can demonstrate the skill steps for our learners. Demonstrating is one of the methods we use to *show* our learners what to do and how to do it.

Perhaps we use laboratory experiences or research projects to provide the learners with experiential learning. In experiential learning, the learners have an opportunity to do the skill steps.

Further, perhaps we use worksheets as practice exercises to help students acquire skills. Practice exercises enable the learners to *repeat* the skills.

Maybe we use simulated "hands-on" experience to assist the learners in transferring their learning from the classroom to real life experiences. These transfer experiences enable the learners to *apply* the skills.

Further, can we define any or all of these teaching methods as skill objectives and develop the skill steps to achieve them? Take another look at your outlines of your specialty contents and determine whether you developed operational steps for implementing your teaching methods.

The Generic Teaching Methods

All of these teaching methods are illustrations of generic teaching methods. (For example, the lecture is just one example of a whole variety of *tell* methods.) Together, we can call these generic teaching methods the *tell-show-do* methods. The *repeat* and *apply* methods may be incorporated under the *do* methods, for they are also forms of participatory kinesthetic experiences.

These generic teaching methods are inclusive: they include all of the methods the teacher requires to deliver his or her content. In addition, these teaching methods respond to the auditory, visual and kinesthetic or the *hear-see-do* needs of the learners. In this context, the teaching methods may be sequenced in an order that will facilitate learning:

Telling the learners what skills to do and how to do them.
Showing the learners how to do the skills.
Doing – providing the learners an opportunity to do the skills.
Repeating – providing the learners with practice exercises for the skills.
Applying – providing real life applications for the skills.

The following are topics of the teaching methods skills learning process.

TELLING – THE DIDACTIC METHODS

Describing The Skill Verbally

Telling is the most common teaching method. For many teachers, the easiest way to deliver skills is to *tell* the learners what they need to know and do. Because It appears to be the easiest method and to require the least energy, the teachers are most comfortable with this mode. In most instances, the teachers lecture to accomplish their teaching objectives.

Telling is essential but not sufficient for your teaching delivery. We *tell* our learners about the new learning.

If they need a fact like the name of an object, we will identify the object: "an internal combustion engine."

If they need a concept like the definition of a new term, we will define the term: "Compression is when the pistons move up in the cylinder, squeezing the fuel and air mixture."

In a like manner, we will *tell* our learners about the principles involved: ". . . exploding gases push the piston down."

Similarly, *telling* our learners how to perform the steps of a skill could include the following: "The first step is to check the spark plugs to see if they need replacement."

We *tell* in a wide variety of ways. These are our *"tell methods."*

Dealing With Words

Using *tell* methods is one of our teaching delivery skills. *Tell* methods answer the question:

"What am I going to use to *tell* my class what they want or need to learn?"

We may select *tell* methods which simply *tell* the learners what they are to learn and how to learn it. For example, there are a variety of *tell* sources available to you: you, another teacher, a learner or a guest speaker. In addition, there is a variety of equipment and/or materials that can be employed by any of these sources to *tell* our learners: audiotapes, videotapes, records, textbooks, worksheets, transparencies or posters.

All of these methods are *tell* methods. While *tell* methods are auditory and tend to benefit the learners with auditory preferences, some are visual. However, all *tell* methods deal with words, either spoken or written.

Expanding Tell Methods

Since we will *tell* our learners what they need to know, we will want to use various *tell* methods. Remember, *tell* methods deal with words, either spoken or written. Here is a list of different teaching methods we can use to *tell*. Add any other *tell* methods you can think of that can give learners the words they need for doing skills.

Tell Methods

Bulletin Board	Interview
Buzz Session	Opaque Projector
Chalkboard	Overhead Projector
Chart	Poster
Checklist	Programmed Instruction

Demonstration	Puppeteering
Discussion	Questioning
Field Trip	Radio
Film	Records
Film Loop	Slides
Filmstrip	Story Telling
Flannel Board	Tapes
Games	Television
Guest Speaker	Testing
Inquiry	Textbooks
	Video Tape

Others:

_____   _____

_____   _____

_____   _____

Telling All Parts Of The Lesson

Telling our learners what it is we want them to do and how to do

CONTENT ORGANIZATION		CONTENT LEVEL	TEACHING METHODS
	R EVIEW	Contingency Skills	Tell
	O VERVIEW	Skill Application	Tell
	P RESENT	Skill Steps	Tell
	E XERCISE	Skill Steps	Tell
	S UMMARIZE	Skill Steps	Tell

it, then, is the first step in our sequence of teaching methods. *Telling* gives our learners an idea of where they are going and how to get there.

In implementing our lesson plans, our *tell* methods address every step of content organization. Thus, we use *tell* methods for all five steps of our *ROPES* lesson plan:

Developing "Tell" Methods

For example, we can use *tell* methods in implementing our presentation of the first skill step, when teaching physical attending:

Presentation

Skill Objective:	The learners will learn to attend physically to the learning experience (teacher and materials) at the highest level of attentiveness (posturing and eye contact).
Skill Step #1:	Square with the teacher and/or learning materials.
Tell Methods:	"We will use the following sub-steps to accomplish the skill step of squaring."

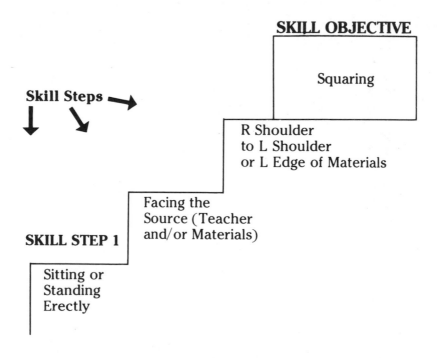

SKILL OBJECTIVE

Squaring

Skill Steps →

R Shoulder
to L Shoulder
or L Edge of Materials

Facing the
Source (Teacher
and/or Materials)

SKILL STEP 1

Sitting or
Standing
Erectly

How many more *tell* methods for the presentation of the skill can you think of?

Designing "Tell" Tasks For The Lesson

The *tell* methods should detail the goal and the steps toward achieving the goal. The learners should find all of the steps they require in their mostly auditory reception of the words of the *tell* method. They should find out what they are going to do and how to do it.

At this point, select a skill objective from one step of your lesson plan and list the first skill step. Then indicate at least one *tell* method that you might employ to orient the learners to the learning tasks.

Skill Objective:
Skill Step #1:
Tell Methods:

How many other *tell* methods can you think of to help orient your learners to the learning tasks?

Orienting The Learners

Telling, then, is the first teaching method: it gives the teacher an opportunity to orient the learners. The *tell* methods simply tell the learners what they are going to learn and how to learn it. The learners, for their part, are supplied with the words to tell them where they are going. They have all of the auditory cues that they will need to guide them to the learning goal.

Tell methods are employed for every skill step at every step of the lesson plan: review, overview, presentation, exercise, and summarize. The *tell* methods give the learners an auditory orientation to the learning tasks which they are about to perform. The learners have systematically developed insights which allow them to proceed on with the learning tasks.

In summary, the *tell* methods deal with words, either spoken or written, which orient the learners to the learning tasks. Reception of the *tell* methods is confidence-building for the learners, because as a result they will know all they need to know in order to proceed in learning.

SHOWING – THE MODELING METHODS

Modeling The Skill

Perhaps the most potent source of teaching is showing. And yet, we are most uncomfortable about showing, because we think it requires great energy and sometimes puts us "on the spot."

Showing is a critical teaching method, because it visually illustrates the skill to be performed. The learners have the opportunity to observe the steps involved in the skills demonstration. Thus, they have not only the meaning of words through *telling*, but also the demonstration of skills through *showing*, to guide them toward their skills performance.

When we *tell* our learners that something is called "an internal combustion engine," we should also *show* them what the engine looks like.

When we explain a concept like the definition of compression, we should *show* our learners a cut-away model or a diagram of the compression cycle.

Before we *tell* our learners about the expansion of the hot gas, we may want to *show* our learners what happens when gas in a container is heated by observing an attached balloon. Our *show* method visually explains the principle our learners need to understand – the power cycle of the engine.

We will also *tell* and *show* the steps of performing the skills. When we *tell* the learners to check the spark plug, we will *show* them how at the same time.

Working With Images

While *tell* methods deal with words, *show* methods deal with pictures. The learners develop mental pictures from the descriptive words we use, or from the pictures we exhibit. The proverb, "A picture is worth a thousand words" is a popular statement of the principle which accounts for the effectiveness of *show* methods, especially for visual learners.

A picture, a diagram, a series of pictures or the action of performing the skills, are what the *show* methods deliver to our learners. The most common *show* method is the demonstration, when the teacher or a learner does the showing.

For example, we may want to teach our learners how to measure the length of a rectangle or splice an electric wire. We may *tell* them how to do it, and *show* them how to do it. We may ask learners who already have the skill to demonstrate. We could use films, slides, pictures, overhead or opaque projectors, posters, models, mock-ups or exhibits to teach the skills with a series of pictures. We can use any one or several of these methods as *show* methods.

Building A Variety of "Show" Methods

Just as we will want to use a variety of *tell* methods, we will want to add variety to our *show* methods. Some of the methods both *tell* and *show* our learners what they need to know. We may use these methods to *tell* and/or *show*. Remember, *show* methods deal in pictures, either live or prepared. List any other *show* methods that give learners a picture of doing the skills:

Show Methods

Bulletin Board
Chalkboard
Chart
Demonstration
Experiments
Field Trip
Film
Film Loop
Filmstrip
Flannel Board
Games
Guest Speaker
Inquiry
Others:

Internship
Model
Mock-up
Opaque Projector
Overhead Projector
Poster
Programmed Instruction
Slides
Story Telling
Television
Textbooks
Video Tapes

_____   _____

_____   _____

Showing All The Content

Showing our learners how to do the skills, then, is the next step in our sequence of teaching methods. *Showing* gives our learners a picture of where they are going and how to get there.

In implementing our lesson plans, our *show* methods address every step of content organization, just as our *tell* methods do. Thus, both *tell* and *show* methods implement all steps of our *ROPES* lesson plan:

	CONTENT LEVEL	TEACHING METHODS
R EVIEW	Contingency Skills	Tell, Show
O VERVIEW	Skill Application	Tell, Show
P RESENT	Skill Steps	Tell, Show
E XERCISE	Skill Steps	Tell, Show
S UMMARIZE	Skill Steps	Tell, Show

(CONTENT ORGANIZATION)

Identifying "Show" Methods

For example, we can use *show* methods in implementing our presentation of the first skill step when teaching physical attending.

Presentation

Skill Objective: The learners will learn to attend physically to the learning experience (teacher and materials) at the highest level of attentiveness (posturing and eye contact).

Skill Step #1: Square with the teacher and/or learning materials.

Show Methods: Teacher demonstrates or uses video tape of:

1. Teacher attending physically to class
   a. Sitting/Standing
   b. Facing source
   c. Squaring with source
2. Teacher attending physically to learner
   a. Sitting/Standing
   b. Facing source
   c. Squaring with source

How many more *show* methods for the presentation of the physical attending skill can you think of?

Designing "Show" Tasks For The Lesson

The *show* methods should provide pictures of the goal and the steps needed to achieve it. The learners should obtain all of the pictures they require from their visual reception of the *show* method. They should have complete pictures of what they are going to do and how to do it.

Now, develop at least one *show* method that you might employ to provide your learners with pictures of their learning tasks:

Skill Objective:
Skill Step #1:
Show Methods:

How many other *show* methods can you think of to help your learners develop pictures of their learning tasks?

Creating Images For The Learners

Showing, then, is the second teaching method: it gives the teacher an opportunity to transmit or stimulate images in the minds of the learners. These images *show* the learners what and how they are going to learn. The learners now have a cognitive map of where they are going.

Just as *tell* methods, *show* methods are employed for every skill step at every stage of the lesson plan. The *show* methods give the learners a visual orientation to the learning tasks they are about to perform. The learners have systematically developed pictures which allow them to proceed and perform the learning tasks.

In summary, the *show methods deal with pictures which orient the learners to the learning tasks. The show* methods give the learners confidence in proceeding to perform the skills, because the learners are guided by their own pictures.

DOING – THE EXPERIENTIAL METHODS

Experiencing The Skill

The most potent source of learning is *doing*. The purpose of the *do* method is to provide learners with the opportunity to experience the skills by *doing* them. *Do* methods involve the learners in the performance of the skills. Often, while teachers are comfortable with their learners *doing* work assignments, they do not understand how to use this method to achieve its full potency.

Do methods are actually learning experiences that the teacher plans so that the learners can participate in or perform the learning. The teacher may also use learning experiences when new words and definitions are introduced. Planning activities which have the learners use facts and concepts will involve them in writing, speaking or drawing. For example, a laboratory that allows the learners to identify a mineral allows students to manipulate a mineral as well as the testing equipment. The learners actually perform the skill of identifying a mineral while learning the supportive knowledge.

Getting The Learners To Participate

We are all kinesthetic learners. While some of us have audio or visual preferences, we all learn by doing. We file permanent images of our behavior when we *do* the skills.

We are providing our learners with an experience when we have each individual perform the skills. The nature of the skills will determine which *do* methods are most appropriate.

The most common *do* method is the worksheet. It provides the teacher with an opportunity to see if the learners know the correct answers. However, many skills cannot be performed on a worksheet because the answers only describe the skill. For these skills, the worksheet is not an appropriate *do* method.

For example, we may want to teach our learners how to brush their teeth. After we have *told* and *shown*, we will want to plan an activity that requires everyone to *do* the skills. This means that we will have to provide each learner with a toothbrush. Then we can plan role-playing, video taping, photography, a contest or a checklist. Using any one or more of these *do* methods, we provide our learners with an experience which has them practicing their skills.

Increasing The Range of "Do" Methods

Introducing variety into our *do* methods is essential to good teaching. Using all of our creative talents, we should expand the *do* methods that our learners will use. If we select a worksheet of twenty questions to do every day, our learners will not be encouraged to practice their skills.

Do methods involve our learners in an experience where they actually use the skills that are to be learned. It is not enough for our learners to tell or show us how they would do the skill. Some of the methods listed below can also be used to *tell* and *show* the skill. List any other *do* methods that give the learners the opportunity to experience *doing* the skills.

Do Methods

Brainstorming	Model
Case Study	News Broadcast
Collection	Oral Report
Colloquium	Panel
Committees	Play
Contests	Practicum
Creative Writing	Project
Debate	Psychodrama
Exhibit	Questionnaire
Fair	Rating Scale
Forum	Research
Games	Role Models
Hands-On	Simulations
Improvisation	Skit
Inventory	Survey
Laboratory	Workshop
Others:	

_____   _____

_____   _____

Experiencing Learning First Hand

Providing our learners with an opportunity to *do* the skills, then, is the next step in our sequence of teaching methods. *Doing* gives our learners the opportunity for a "hands-on" experience of the skills.

In implementing our lesson plan, our *do* methods address every step of content organization just as do our *tell* and *show* methods. Thus, *tell*, *show* and *do* methods implement all steps of our *ROPES* lesson plan.

CONTENT ORGANIZATION		CONTENT LEVEL	TEACHING METHODS
R EVIEW		Contingency Skills	Tell, Show, Do
O VERVIEW		Skill Application	Tell, Show, Do
P RESENT		Skill Steps	Tell, Show, Do
E XERCISE		Skill Steps	Tell, Show, Do
S UMMARIZE		Skill Steps	Tell, Show, Do

Discriminating "Do" Methods

For example, we can use *do* methods in implementing our presentation of the first skill step when teaching physical attending.

Presentation

Skill Objective: The learners will learn to attend physically to the learning experience (teacher and materials) at the highest level of attentiveness (posturing and eye contact).

Skill Step #1: Square with the teacher and learning materials.

Do Methods Learner demonstrates following skills:
1. Attending physically to teacher

a. Sitting/Standing
b. Facing source
2. Attending physically to learning material
a. Sitting/Standing
b. Facing source
c. Squaring with source

How many more *do* methods for the presentation of the physical attending skill can you think of?

Developing "Do" Tasks For The Lesson

The *do* methods should provide the learners with the experience of performing the skills. The learners should have a complete experience of *doing* the skills.

Now, develop at least one *do* method that you might employ to provide your learners with the experience of performing the skill:

Skill Objective:

Skill Step #1:
Do Methods:

How many other *do* methods can you think of to help your learners experience doing the skills?

Learning Is Performing

Doing, then, is the third teaching method: the learners' actual performance of the skills. The learners have a direct experience in *doing* the skills. The learners have now demonstrated that they can do the skills.

Just as with *tell* and *show* methods, *do* methods are employed at every step of the lesson plan. The *do* methods are the actual demonstration by the learners of their performance of the skills.

In summary, the *do* methods involve the actual physical performance of the skills. The performance is observable and measurable. The *do* methods give the learners confidence in their ability to acquire the skills.

REPEATING – THE PRACTICE METHODS

Practicing The Skill

Doing demonstrates acquisition. *Repeating* insures acquisition.

Repeat methods are just what the label suggests: methods which repeat the skill steps. They involve practice exercises that enable the learners to retain the skill through repetition. While teachers are usually comfortable with their learners' being occupied in doing practice exercises, use of the exercises is sometimes more for their benefit than for that of the learners.

However, it is necessary for the learners to *repeat* the skill by itself. This way the learners can concentrate upon performing the skill steps of the new skill. Suppose, for example, the new skill is writing a complete sentence. Some methods that could be used for repeat exercises include committees, contests, games, written questions and worksheets.

One illustration of a way to plan the repeat exercises is to have the learners form committees (method) and to answer questions (method) using complete sentences (skill). In this manner, the learners would be repeating only one skill. It would not be appropriate to have the learners use creative writing at this time. If they did, they would have to use other skills such as writing a topic sentence and writing a paragraph as well as writing complete sentences.

Repeating is Telling, Showing and Doing

Repeating is really the learners' *tell-show-do*. The teachers *told* them and *showed* them what to do and how to do it. Then the teachers provided them with the opportunity to *do* it.

In *doing* the skill, the learners have the opportunity to *tell-show-do* their own learning experience. While they are performing the skill (*do*), they can present the words (*tell*) and the pictures (*show*) concerning the performance of the skill.

Once we have selected the *repeat* methods of the exercise, we can consider ways that the learners will *repeat* the skill within these methods. It would not be sufficient practice for the learners to write one sentence, or print ''i'' once, or add one example. We should expand the repetitions within the method as carefully as we selected the method.

Expanding "Repeat" Methods

We need to answer the question: "How many different ways can our learners *repeat* the skills using the methods we have selected?" We can list the examples or items that require the learners to *repeat* the new skill within the chosen methods.

We can use the list of methods below to find several *do* methods that the learners could use just to *repeat* the new skills. Remember that we will not want the learners to use more than one skill in the *repeat* exercise. Look over the list and add any other *repeat* methods that can insure learner acquisition of skills.

Repeat Methods

Chart	Play
Collection	Poster Making
Committees	Projects
Contests	Questions
Creative Writing	Reports
Debate	Research
Discussion	Simulations
Exhibit	Skit
Fair	Story Telling
Forum	Tape Making
Games	Transparency Making
Oral Report	Worksheets
Panel	Workshops
Others:	

_____   _____

_____   _____

_____   _____

Repeating In The Exercise

Providing the learners with an opportunity to *repeat* the skills, then, is the next step in our sequence of teaching methods. *Repeating* gives our learners the opportunity to practice the skills.

In implementing our lesson plan, *repeat* methods address only the "exercise" step of content organization. Thus, the *repeat* methods follow the *tell-show-do* methods only during the exercise of the skills.

CONTENT ORGANIZATION		CONTENT LEVEL	TEACHING METHODS
	R EVIEW	Contingency Skills	Tell, Show, Do
	O VERVIEW	Skill Application	Tell, Show, Do
	P RESENT	Skill Steps	Tell, Show, Do
	E XERCISE	Skill Steps	Tell, Show, Do, Repeat
	S UMMARIZE	Skill Steps	Tell, Show, Do, Do

Sampling The "Repeat" Methods

For example, we can use *repeat* methods in implementing our presentation of the first skill step when teaching physical attending.

Presentation

Skill Objective: The learners will learn to attend physically to the learning experience (teacher and materials) at the highest level of attentiveness (posturing and eye contact).

Skill Step #1: Square with the teacher and learning materials

Repeat Methods: Learners repeat the following skills in at least five different positions:

1. Attending physically to individuals and groups of students
   a. Sitting/Standing
   b. Facing source
   c. Squaring with source
2. Attending physically to homework
   a. Sitting/Standing
   b. Facing source
   c. Squaring with source

How many more *repeat* methods for the presentation of the physical attending skill can you think of?

Constructing "Repeat" Tasks For The Lesson

The *repeat* methods provide learners with the opportunity to exercise the skills. The learners have the practice experience necessary to insure skills acquisition.

Now, develop at least one *repeat* method that you might employ to provide your learners with the opportunity to practice the skills.

Skill Objective:

Skill Step #1:
Repeat Methods:

How many other *repeat* methods can you think of to help insure your learners' success?

Repeating Ensures Learning

Repeating, then, is the fourth teaching method: the learners' practice of the skill. The learners repeat the skills over and over in the context of different *tell-show-do* methods. In reality, *repeating* is the learners' *tell-show-do*: the learner *tells* and *shows* as he or she *does* the skills.

Unlike the *tell-show-do* methods, however, the *repeat* methods are employed only during the exercise step of content organization. Thus, the learners' *tell-show-do* takes place following the teacher's *tell-show-do* during the exercise.

In summary, the *repeat* methods are the learners' insurance policy for skill acquisition. The *repeat* methods give the learners confidence in their ability to produce the skills upon the presentation of appropriate stimuli.

APPLYING – THE TRANSFER METHODS

Using The Skill in Real Life

Applying is yet another phase of *doing*. *Applying* is the ultimate purpose of the skills the learners have acquired. *Applying* methods involve the uses or outcomes to which skills are put. They involve the generalization or transfer of learning from the acquired skill to the applied skill. Most teachers are very uncomfortable with the *applying* method, because they have not been taught how to help their learners to transfer their learnings.

After the learners have acquired and practiced the skills, they must learn to apply the skills. They must learn to take the skills back to the contexts or environments from which they came. The learners should be able to make more effective applications than they could prior to learning the new skills.

For example, at some point in history, the needs for computational skills were diagnosed. The intervening teaching process taught the learners these skills. The test of the effectiveness of the teaching is the learners' application of the skills in real life. The more effective is the application of the skills, the more effective was the teaching.

Dealing With Mastery

A very important requirement of writing *apply* exercises is to be certain that the learners have already mastered all of the old skills they will be expected to use within the application. This insures success with the task and mastery of the new skill. The learners will be confident of their performance, and thus free to learn what you are teaching.

For example, when teaching the skill of writing a complete sentence, you could select writing a paragraph as an application, if the learners have already learned how to write a paragraph. Some *apply* methods that could be used for applications are creative writing, current events, oral reports and story telling. To practice the skill of writing complete sentences, the learners could write a paragraph (application) on a current event topic (method) and then give a brief oral report (method) speaking in complete sentences (skill).

Varying The Applications

After the learners have performed the skill in the *repeat* exercises, then, they will need to *apply* the skill. To write the *apply* exercises, we must answer the question, "What applications should my learners use to practice the skill?"

After you have a list of *applications* for each skill, you will want to write the methods for practicing the *applications*. Choosing the methods used in *applied* exercises is accomplished in the same manner as choosing the *repeat* exercises. You can review the list of *apply* methods with respect to the applications you wrote. If possible, you should try to select a variety of apply methods. Add any other apply *methods you can think of.*

Apply Methods

Brainstorming	Panel
Case Study	Play
Collection	Poster Making
Colloquium	Practicum
Committees	Project
Contests	Psychodrama
Creative Writing	Questions
Current Events	Rating Scale
Debate	Reports
Exhibit	Research
Fair	Role Models
Forum	Simulations
Games	Skits
Hands-On Improvisation	Story Telling

Inventory
Laboratory
Model
Oral Report
Others:

Survey
Worksheets
Workshops

_____   _____

_____   _____

_____   _____

Providing Opportunities To Apply

Providing the learners with an opportunity to *apply* the skills in a real life context, then, is the next step in our sequence of teaching methods. *Applying* methods insure the successful applica-

CONTENT ORGANIZATION		CONTENT LEVEL	TEACHING METHODS
	R EVIEW	Contingency Skills	Tell, Show, Do
	O VERVIEW	Skill Application	Tell, Show, Do
	P RESENT	Skill Steps	Tell, Show, Do
	E XERCISE	Skill Steps	Tell, Show, Do, Repeat, Apply
	S UMMARIZE	Skill Steps	Tell, Show, Do,

tion of the skills.

In implementing our lesson plan, our *apply* methods address only the "exercise" step of content organization. In this respect, the *apply* methods follow and duplicate the repeat methods during the exercise of the skills.

Identifying Applications

For example, we can use *apply* methods in implementing our presentation of the first skill step when teaching physical attending.

Presentation

Skill Objective: The learners will learn to attend physically to the learning experience (teacher and materials) at the highest level of attentiveness (posturing and eye contact).

Skill Step #1: Square with the teacher and learning materials.

Apply Methods: Learners repeat following skills:
1. Attending physically to people in home, community and work environments:
    a. Sitting/Standing
    b. Facing source
    c. Squaring with source
2. Attending physically to learning materials in home, community and work environments:
    a. Sitting/Standing
    b. Facing source
    c. Squaring with source

How many more *apply* methods for the presentation of the physical attending skill can you think of?

Designing "Apply" Tasks For The Lesson

The *apply* methods provide the learners with the opportunity to use the skill in a real life context. The learners have the practical

applications necessary to insure the utility of the skills application.
Now, develop at least one *apply* method that you might
employ to provide your learners with the opportunity to apply the
skills.

Skill Objective:

Skill Step #1:
Apply Methods:

How many other *apply* methods can you think of to help
insure your learners' skill application?

Using What Is Learned

Applying, then, is the fifth teaching method: it gives the
learners the opportunity to apply the skills. The learners *apply* the
skill in real living, learning and working situations.
Like the *repeat* methods, the *apply* methods are employed
exclusively during the exercise step of content organization. Thus,
the learners either make the *application*, or they do not. Teaching is
successful, or it is not.
In summary, the *apply* methods accomplish the outcome of
the teaching process: the application to which the skills will be put
in a real-life context. The *apply* methods give the learners confidence in their ability to use the skills upon demand.

SUMMARIZING
TEACHING METHODS

Putting It Together

Expertise in our teaching methods is what publicly identifies
us as teachers. The point of learner involvement with both the
teachers and the content, is the teaching method which the teacher
uses to deliver the content. The methods that we use to involve our
learners in learning reflect our own unique approaches to delivering

content. We are "how" we teach.

At this point, you may wish to consider again the important teaching methods. Only now, instead of deriving random benefits from the variety principle, you can organize and sequence the generic teaching methods systematically. In addition, each generic method has an extensive back-up of specific teaching methods that can be individualized for the learners' unique needs.

Outline any teaching methods and relevant supportive knowledge that you would employ in delivering your content. Use your content development skills to define the teaching methods.

Skill Steps: _____   _____   _____ _____

Skill Objective: _____   _____   _____ _____

Principle: _____   _____   _____ _____

Concept: _____   _____   _____ _____

Facts: _____   _____   _____ _____

Checking Out Your Methods

You may wish again to take a skill in your specialty content, and outline how you would organize your teaching system now. Use the teaching skills which you have already learned. Only this time, reproduce the teaching system yourselves. This way, you will get an index of how well you have learned your teaching methods.

_____

_____

_____

_____

_____

_____

Reviewing The Alternatives

Within each of the steps of content organization, we can use the generic *tell-show-do* teaching methods:

Telling the learners what skills to perform and how to perform them.

Showing the learners how to do the skills.

Doing – providing the learners an opportunity to do the skills.

In addition, within the exercise step of content organization, teachers must provide the learners with the opportunity to *tell-show-do* in the repeat and apply exercises:

Repeating – providing the learners with practice exercises for the skills.

Applying – providing real life applications for the skills.

If we have incorporated all of these generic methods in the delivery of our content, then we can achieve our own personal skill objective of applying our teaching methods. If we can implement the specific teaching methods in our specialty content, then we can deliver our content to our learners.

CONTENT ORGANIZATION	CONTENT LEVEL	TEACHING METHODS
REVIEW	Contingency Skills	Tell, Show, Do
OVERVIEW	Skill Application	Tell, Show, Do
PRESENT	Skill Steps	Tell, Show, Do
EXERCISE	Skill Steps	Tell, Show, Do, Repeat, Apply
SUMMARIZE	Skill Steps	**Tell, Show, Do, Repeat, Apply**

Humanizing Learning

Together, the generic teaching methods, used in conjunction with the steps of content organization, parallel our learners' involvement in the learning process.

Reviewing the content involves using *tell-show-do* teaching methods to diagnose the contingency skills. Then the learners will know what they can and cannot do. The learners can explore where they are in relation to the new learning tasks.

Overviewing the content involves using *tell-show-do* teaching methods to teach the potential skill applications. Then the learners will know when to use the skill. They can understand where they are in relation to where they want to be with the learning tasks.

Presenting the content involves using *tell-show-do* teaching methods to teach the skill steps. Then the learners will know how to do the skill. They can act to get from where they are to where they want to be with the learning tasks.

Exercising the content involves using *repeat* and *apply* teaching methods as well as *tell-show-do* teaching methods to practice the skill. This reinforces the learners' acting to achieve their learning goals.

Summarizing the content involves using *tell-show-do* teaching methods to provide the learners with an opportunity to demonstrate what they have learned. Thus, the learners have another chance to experientially engage the skill. They can complete their acting to achieve their learning goals.

Making Teaching Effective

Yes, there are as many different kinds of teaching as there are teachers. And yes, our teaching methods reflect the uniqueness of our personal development. That is exhilarating! But no, not all teachers have effective teaching methods, however individualized to their own particular talents their methods are.

The point is simply this: it is not the individualization of teaching methods to the *teacher's* talents that is the critical source of effectiveness; it is the individualization of teaching methods to the *learners'* talents.

The *tell-show-do* teaching methods meet the learners' *hear-see-do* needs for acquiring new skills. In addition, the learners have their own opportunity to *tell-show-do* their learning, during the *repeat* and *apply* stages of the exercise and summary steps of

117

content organization. Thus, the learners have the critical role in their own learning. The learners learn to be their own best teachers.

RESEARCH BACKGROUND: TEACHING METHODS

The Sources of Effectiveness in Methods

The sources of all learning in all human relationships are the same. First, the "more knowing" person has something that the "less knowing" person wants or needs. Second, the "more knowing" person relates to the "less knowing" person's needs from both an internal and an external frame of reference; internal in terms of the learner's reference; external, in terms of the content. Third, the "more knowing" person works in conjunction with the "less knowing" person to develop a programmatic way to get the learner to achieve what he or she wants or needs.

These sources are the same for all helping and human relationships: parent-child; teacher-student; counselor-counselee; health care worker-patient; employer-employee. We may conceive of them as the modeling, experiential and didactic sources of learning. In modeling learning, we teach by behaving and doing things that others want to be able to do. In experiential learning, we provide others with the opportunity to do these things. In didactic learning, we do all those things that enable the learners to do what they want or need to do.

Modeling is most fundamental in motivating the learner. Experiencing is the learning itself. Didacticism is the method by which we accomplish the learning. The teaching methods are incorporated here.

All teaching methods must lead to experiential learning. The learners only file permanent images of their learning after they have had repeated kinesthetic experiences, i.e, after they have practiced the skills that define the learning.

The Principle of Effective Methods

The question, then, is what kinds of didactic experiences lead to experiential learning? If the experiential learning is the actual doing of the skills, then the skills must be modeled or shown by the teacher's doing. If the skills are modeled by the teacher, then the teacher must also tell about them as they are shown.

In general, research suggests that teachers who employ a variety of methods are effective. When these methods, in turn, utilize the different sensory modalities, the teachers are most effective. In this context, those teachers are most effective who employ a variety of didactic methods that tell the learners what to do and how to do it; demonstration methods that show learners how to do it; and experiential methods that provide the learners with an opportunity to do it. The basic principle of teaching methods is that all effective teaching methods emphasize kinesthetic learning.

In this regard, research suggests that students learn from a variety of teaching methods. For example, students tend to acquire more factual knowledge from lectures and "higher level thinking" from discussion methods (Dubin and Taveggia, 1968; McKeachie and Kulik, 1975). The same is true of other teaching methods: tutoring; use of printed material in seatwork and homework; simulations and games, and television or film (Gage, 1976). Each of these methods can make important contributions to classroom instruction. The critical variable with many of these methods appears to be time: the students tend to learn best what they spend the most time doing (Berliner, 1977).

In general, the purpose of the teacher in utilizing teaching methods is to maximize student involvement in learning: it is "aimed at bringing the students into effective interaction with the instructional materials, with a maximum of engaged learning time." (Gage, 1977) In other words, the more time the students spend doing the tasks, the more they learn.

In this context, it has been suggested that skillful teachers can teach across different contents because their knowledge of the subject matter needs are adequate to the task of supplementing the instructional materials with which the students are working (Gage, 1977). Even at the secondary level, the teacher's role becomes similar across different contents, because the complexities specific to teaching the contents are handled by instructional materials. In other words, the skillful teacher becomes "a humane facilitator of student interaction with instructional material." Thus, generic teaching methods may be most effective in helping students to use specialized teaching materials.

The Quality of Variety

It would seem that utilizing combinations of methods and materials would have the effect of a multi-method approach. The presentation of information would have a higher probability of coinciding with the learner's modal learning preference (Berenson, 1978; Kaya, et al, 1967). In other words, the learners have different sensory learning preferences. By employing the "variety principle" and presenting methods utilizing a variety of sensory modalities, the teachers can become most effective in bringing the learners into maximum contact with the learning experience.

Summary of Research Findings

In summary, the generic teaching methods presented (Chapter 4) give attention to all of the sensory modalities of the learners (Berenson, Berenson and Carkhuff, 1978). Thus, the telling or didactic methods reach the learners through auditory modalities; the showing or modeling methods reach the learners through visual modalities; the doing or experiential methods reach the learners through kinesthetic modalities. Together, the tell-show-do methods are inclusive, and maximize the attention to the kinesthetic learning. The teaching methods described offer a comprehensive approach to the development of instructional methods.

In conclusion, of the telling, showing and doing methods, the doing are most fundamental because they represent the actual performance of the skill by which we define our learning. However, when we increase the variety of not only the do, but also the tell and show methods, we increase the probability of learner acquisition and application and, ultimately, the transfer of learning.

References

Berenson, D. H. "The Teacher in the Learning Equation," in *Toward Excellence in Education*, R. R. Carkhuff and J.W. Becker, eds. Amherst, Mass.: Carkhuff Institute of Human Technology, 1978.

Berenson, D. H., Berenson, Sarah R. and Carkhuff, R. R. *The Skills of Teaching - Lesson Planning Skills*. Amherst, Mass.: Human Resource Development Press, 1978.

Berliner, D. C. *Instructional Time in Research on Teaching*. San Francisco, Calif.: Far West Laboratory for Educational Research and Development, 1977.

Dubin, R. and Taveggia, T. C. *The Teaching-Learning Paradox: A Comparative Analysis of College Teaching Methods*. Eugene, Or.: Center for the Advanced Study of Educational Administration, University of Oregon, 1968.

Gage, N. L., ed. *The Psychology of Teaching Methods: The 75th Yearbook of the National Society for the Study of Education*. Part I. Chicago, Ill.: University of Chicago Press, 1976.

Gage, N. L. *The Scientific Basis of the Art of Teaching*. New York, N.Y.: Teachers College Press, 1977.

Kaya, E., Gerhard, M., Stasiewski, A. and Berenson, D. H. *Developing a Theory of Educational Practices for the Elementary School*. Norwalk, Conn.: Ford Foundation Fund for the Improvement of Education, 1967.

McKeachie, W. J. and Kulik, J. A. "Effective College Teaching," in *Review of Research on Education, Vol. 3.*, F. N. Kerlingler, ed. Itasca, Ill.: F. E. Peacock, 1975.

Teaching
Delivery Skills   5

DEVELOPING
AN EFFECTIVE
DELIVERY

Deliveries We Have Known

How many of us remember being on the receiving end of the teaching delivery? Our teacher consulted the lesson plan. It had been developed and refined with years of experience. It dictated the day's learning tasks.

Sometimes it was passed on from a previous teacher or copied from a supervising teacher. Always, it was consulted by the substitute teachers. Indeed, we used to joke that if we removed it, our teacher would not know what to do.

Perhaps we were miserable in school because the lesson plan – and not the students – was the overriding factor in the teaching equation. The curriculum proceeded independent of us. It had a life of its own, and our classroom activities revolved around it. Day by day, week by week, the curriculum moved inexorably to its conclusion, not necessarily to our learning. No wonder we felt so happy to get out of school in June.

Delivery Skills – Teaching Skills

Many teachers teach content. Effective teachers teach learners.

The difference between those who teach content and those who teach learners is in their teaching delivery skills.

For most of us, the teaching delivery is the most intense and rewarding moment in teaching, because it brings the teacher into direct contact with the learners. We have developed our content to deliver to our learners. We have prepared our lesson plans and methods for delivery. Now we funnel our content, lesson plans and teaching methods through the learning process in which we involve our learners.

Again, the learning process involves the learners in *exploring* where they are with the content; *understanding* where they are in relation to where they want or need to be; and *acting* to get from where they are to where they want or need to be. The delivery skills facilitate the learners' movement through these phases of learning.

An Assessment of Your Delivery

The problem is that many times we emphasize our content without understanding its impact upon the learners. Often our content is not responsive to the learners' needs. Steps are missing in its development and organization. We will fill in these missing steps with our teaching delivery.

At this time, it may be helpful to consider for a moment some of the delivery skills which you employ in your direct contacts with learners. What are some of these teaching delivery skills and what do they do for you in teaching? What are the principles which govern their effectiveness? How can they be defined as skills? How can you break out the skill steps to achieve skills?

Teaching Delivery Skills

Skill Steps:	____	____	____	____	____
Skill Objective:	____	____	____	____	____
Principle:	____	____	____	____	____
Concept:	____	____	____	____	____
Facts:	____	____	____	____	____

At this point, it may also be helpful to get an index of your previous learning about teaching delivery skills. Perhaps you can again take a skill in your specialty content and outline the methods you would employ to deliver it. In so doing, orient your skills toward the learners' movement through the learning process. What delivery skills do you employ to facilitate the learners' movement through each of the phases of learning?

PHASES OF LEARNING		LEARNING PROCESS	TEACHING DELIVERY SKILLS
	PRE-LEARNING	Involvement	_____
			_____
	1	Exploring	_____
			_____
	2	Understanding	_____
			_____
	3	Acting	_____
			_____
	POST-LEARNING	Recycling	_____
			_____

The Ingredients of An Effective Delivery

This task may appear difficult. The first consideration, then, is to have *prepared our content*. However, there are several sets of delivery skills with which we are already familiar. Later, we will find how really simple teaching delivery is if we have prepared our content properly.

In this context, we are all familiar with the need to *diagnose* the learners' levels of functioning with the content we have prepared. We recognize that the more accurate are our discriminations of the learners' functioning, the more effectively we can teach them.

Diagnosis leads to a consideration of education *goals* and *objectives*. Do we *diagnose* and *set goals* in a moment-to-moment manner? Or are our goals predetermined?

The same questions can be asked with regard to the instruction which we deliver to achieve our *goals*: is it related to the *diagnosis* of where the learners are functioning or is it predetermined? Is it broken down *programmatically* into small steps that enable the learners to achieve the goals?

Finally, we might want to ask whether we have monitored the *feedback* which the learners receive from their performance. This *feedback* will recycle the phases of learning: more extensive exploration; more accurate understanding; more effective action.

The essential question for us is whether we can define any or all of our concepts of teaching delivery skills as skill objectives and skill steps. Take another look at your outlines of your specialty contents and determine whether you have developed operational steps for implementing your delivery skills.

The Delivery Model

All of these delivery skills are illustrations of generic teaching delivery skills. These generic teaching delivery skills are inclusive: they include all of the skills the teacher requires to deliver the content to the learners. They enable the teacher to guide the learners from where they are to where they want to be in the learning experience. These teaching delivery skills can be sequenced in an order that will facilitate learning:

> **Content preparation**, or preparing the daily content of skills;
> **Diagnosing** the learners' levels of functioning on the skills, and their knowledge of the daily content;
> **Goal-setting** for the skills and knowledge objectives, based upon the diagnosis of the learners;
> **Programming**, or developing programs to achieve the skills and knowledge goals of the learners;
> **Monitoring**, or observing the feedback which the learners receive from acting upon the learning programs.

These are the topics of the teaching delivery skills learning that follows.

The Principle of An Effective Delivery

What was so frustrating to us in our school days was that we could not handle the learning because some of the steps were too large for us. We did not get it right the first time around. Yet there was no second chance. Nor were the steps made smaller.

Even if we failed the test, we were moved on to the next set of teaching objectives as dictated by the curriculum or text. It did not matter how we performed – the content was going to move on without us.

Now we are the teachers. The fundamental question for us is this: are we going to break down our teaching units in steps small enough for each learner? The answer to this question is particularly critical because the fundamental principle of teaching delivery is this: *all effective teaching is broken down in atomistic steps*. The delivery skills that can be used to fulfill this principle are the topics of this chapter.

PREPARING THE CONTENT

Getting Ready for Delivery

We have already attended to content preparation in our first three sets of learning skills. We have developed our content, and planned our lessons and teaching methods before we come into contact with the learners in the delivery phase of teaching. In other words, content preparation takes place before learning ensues.

Thus, we can see (following in an abbreviated form) that content preparation is funnelled into the teaching-learning process during the prelearning phase. See if you can fill in the words that fit the abbreviations.

Using the Learning Model

The relationship between the prepared content and the phases of teaching delivery is important to understand. The explora-

PHASES OF LEARNING · **PRE-LEARNING PHASE**

TEACHING DELIVERY SKILLS

Content Organization:	R	O	P	E	S
Content Level:	CS	SA	SS	SS	SS
Teaching Methods:	T S D	T S D	T S D	T S^R D^A	T S D

PREPARING CONTENT

tion-understanding-acting (E-U-A) learning process, upon which teaching delivery is based, is an ongoing one. In other words, within every stage of the lesson plan, the E-U-A process is recycled for the learners. The teacher is constantly diagnosing, setting goals, programming and monitoring in order to facilitate the learners' E-U-A process.

Thus, for example, within the review of contingency skills, the teacher is using delivery skills to facilitate the E-U-A process. Teaching delivery skills involve moment-to-moment programming for learning achievement. They make the learning process live. They make the lesson plan work.

DIAGNOSING THE LEARNERS

Determining Learner Entry Level

Diagnosing the learner is where the teaching delivery begins. The diagnosis lets us know where the learners are functioning in terms of the skills content. It also lets the learners know where they are beginning their learning experiences.

By letting both teacher and learners know the point of the learners' entry into the learning experience, the diagnosis allows them to detail the teaching goals and programs. Most important, it allows both teacher and learners to tailor the learning of the content to the learners' unique needs. In other words, an accurate diagnosis is the basis for individualizing the learning process in terms of the learners' abilities to perform the skills content.

Facilitating Learner Exploration

In short, the diagnosis tells us the degrees of latitude and longitude from which the individual learners embark upon their learning journey. It enables us to determine precisely the degrees of latitude and longitude which we seek to achieve at our point of destination.

Thus, the diagnostic process facilitates the learners' essential movement through the exploration phase of learning: exploring where they are in relation to the skills content. This provides the necessary conditions for movement to the next phase of learning: setting goals in order to facilitate the learners' understanding of where they are in relation to where they want or need to be.

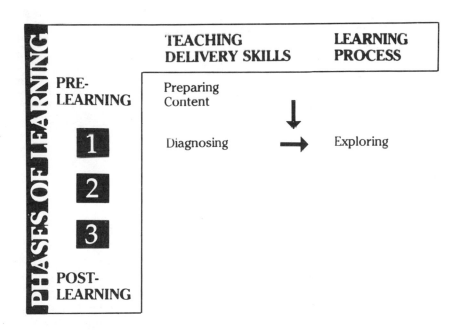

Assessing Skills

The essential question in diagnosis is; can the individual learners perform the skill? The implementation of the review enables us to make this functional diagnosis. If the learners can perform the skill, then they are ready to learn the next skill. For example, if the learners can attend physically, then they are ready to learn the skills involved in observing the learning experience.

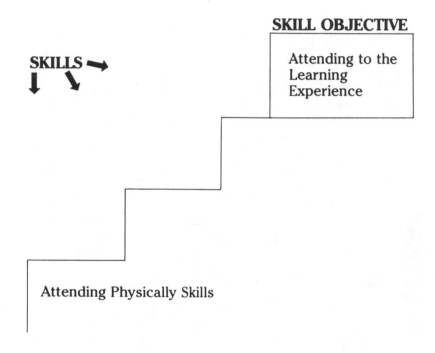

Diagnosing Skills Step Performance

If, on the other hand, the learners cannot perform the skill, then we must discriminate the things they can do from those they cannot. After discrimination of skill performance, then, we must discriminate skill step performance. In other words, we must determine the number of steps which the learners can perform on the way to achievement of the skill. For example, if we are teaching attending physically as our learning skill objective, we may diagnose that an individual learner cannot perform the squaring skill step. The level at which the learners perform the skill steps dictates the level at which we set the next skill objective.

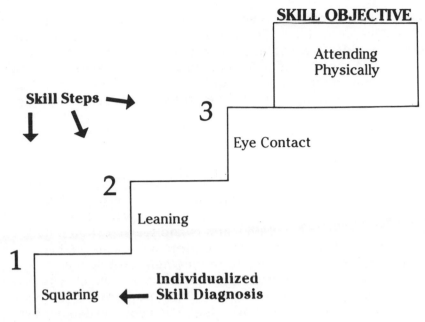

Surveying Supportive Knowledge

If the learners cannot perform a given skill step, it may be because they lack the supportive knowledge. The next stage of

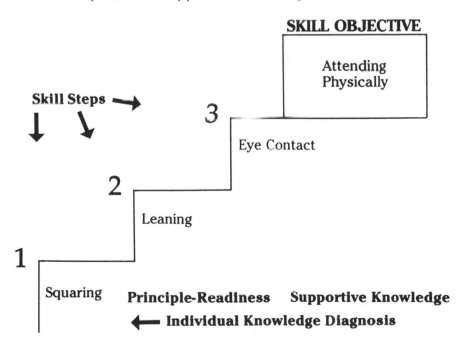

diagnosing the learners, then, involves a diagnosis of their level of supportive knowledge. The learners may lack the facts and/or concepts and/or principles needed to perform the skill steps. For example, in the attending learning program, the learner may lack the principle of readiness for learning that derives from squaring: if the learners attend physically, then they are ready for learning.

Devising Diagnostic Tasks

The diagnosis should describe the learners' level of functioning with regard to the skills and skill steps as well as the supportive knowledge. Both learners and teacher should have an observable index of the learners' performance. This enables both to know the point of entry into the learning experience.

At this point, select a skill objective for which you have developed your lesson plan and teaching methods. Develop your skill steps and supportive knowledge so that you can diagnose your learners' levels of functioning.

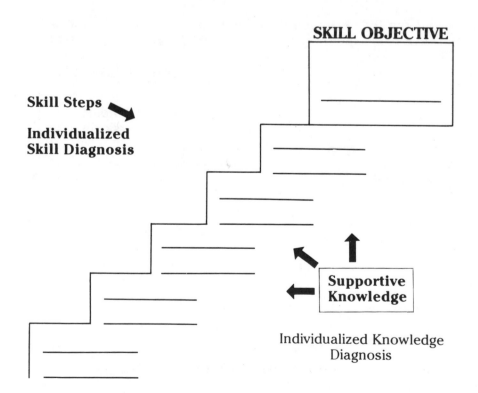

SKILL OBJECTIVE

Skill Steps

Individualized
Skill Diagnosis

Supportive
Knowledge

Individualized Knowledge
Diagnosis

Diagnosing Is Exploring

All teaching preparation, including the content, lesson plans and methods, is processed through the phases of learning in which the learner is engaged. The first of these phases is the learners' exploration of where they are in relation to the skills and knowledge of the content. The teacher facilitates the learners' movement through exploration by using diagnostic skills.

Diagnosing, then, is the second step of direct contact between teacher and learners that takes place during the teaching delivery. It gives both teacher and learners precise and first-hand knowledge of the learners' initial level of functioning.

Perhaps most important, it gives both teacher and learners confidence in the ensuing teaching-learning process.

SETTING LEARNING GOALS

Identifying What Is Needed

The purpose of the diagnosis is to set goals for the learners. The diagnosis lets us know where the learners are functioning in terms of the skills content. Goal-setting lets us know where the learners are going to learn to function.

Our goal-setting skills enable us to define and detail the learners' goals and objectives. The goals and objectives are within the grasp of the learners, because they are based upon accurate diagnoses of the learners. Most important, goal-setting enables both teacher and learners to focus upon goals that are tailored to the learners' unique needs.

Facilitating Learner Understanding

Again, the point of origin as well as the destination of the learning experience is known to the learners due to the teacher's diagnostic and goal-setting skills. The unique needs of the learners can be met in their special learning programs.

Thus, our goal-setting process facilitates the learners' essential movement through the understanding phase of learning: understanding where they are in relation to where they want or need to be with the skills content. This provides the necessary conditions for movement to the next phase of learning: developing programs in order to facilitate the learners' action programs, to get them from where they are to where they want or need to be with the skills content.

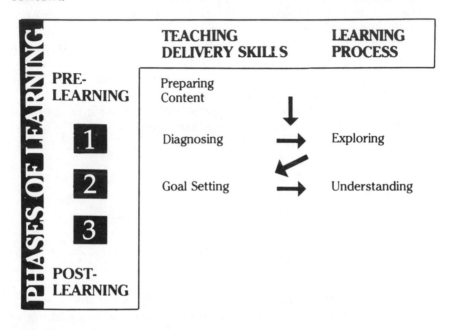

Setting Skill Objectives

The essential question of goal-setting is similar to the diagnostic question: can the learners potentially perform the skill? Obviously, the answer is based upon the skill diagnosis. Diagnosis of the learners' ability to perform the skill will determine the next level of skills goals. For example, if the learners cannot attend physically to the learning experience, then attending physically becomes or remains the skill goal. The overview is the primary phase within which the goal setting activities of the teacher and the learners should take place.

Developing Skill Step Objectives

After we have discriminated the skill performance of the learners, we must determine the next level of skill steps that the

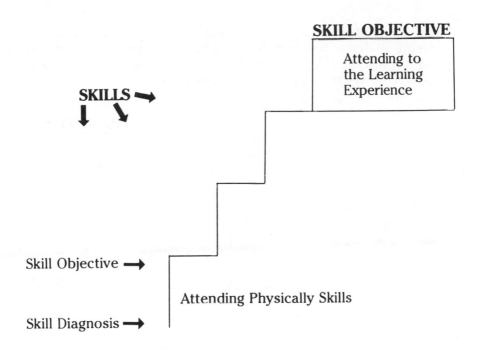

SKILLS →

SKILL OBJECTIVE

Attending to
the Learning
Experience

Skill Objective →

Attending Physically Skills

Skill Diagnosis →

learners can learn to perform. For example, if we are teaching attending physically as our learning skill objective, we may set an

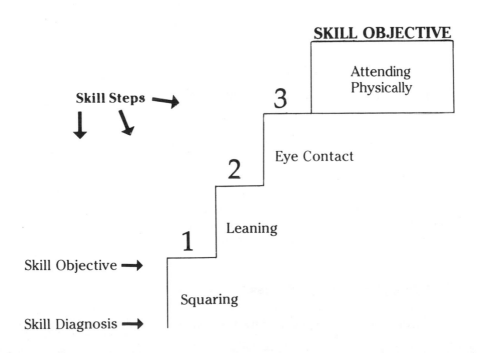

Skill Steps →

SKILL OBJECTIVE

Attending
Physically

3

Eye Contact

2

Leaning

1

Skill Objective →

Squaring

Skill Diagnosis →

objective of squaring for individual learners whom we diagnose as being unable to perform the squaring skill step. Again, the level at which the learners perform the skill steps dictates the level at which we set the next skill step objective.

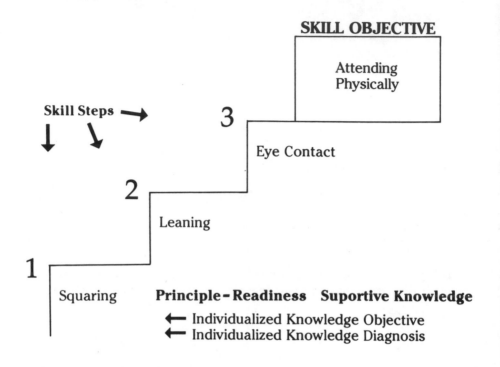

Planning Supportive Knowledge Goals

If learners cannot perform a given skill step because they lack the supportive knowledge, then we must set goals for learning the supportive knowledge. For example, if the learners lack comprehension of the principle of readiness in learning the squaring skill step, then the principle of readiness becomes the supportive-knowledge goal; if the learners square with the learning experience, then they will be prepared to attend physically, so that they will see and hear the teacher and the learning materials.

Designing Goal-Setting Tasks

Goal-setting should define the learners' target level of functioning for skills and knowledge. Both learners and teacher must have observable goals, and objectives that both will know have been achieved. Thus, both will be able to identify the point of exit from the learning experience.

At this point, again use the skill objective for which you have developed your lesson plan and teaching methods. Develop goals for your skill steps and supportive knowledge depending upon your diagnosis of the learners' levels of functioning. Simply note the skill objective based upon the diagnosis of the individual learners' performances.

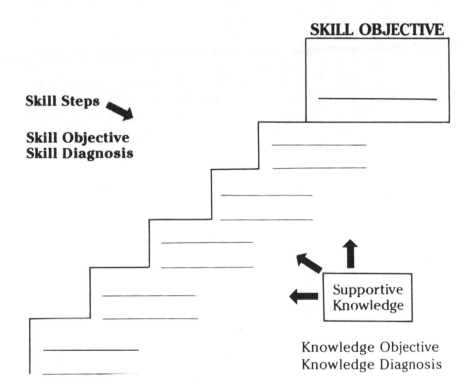

Goal Setting Is Understanding

Again, all content preparation is processed through the phases of learning. After using their diagnostic skills to facilitate the learners' exploration of where they are in relation to the content, the teachers now use their goal-setting skills to facilitate the learners' understanding of where they want or need to be.

PROGRAMMING FOR SUCCESS

Developing Learning Programs

The purpose of the learning program is to help the learners to achieve the learning goals. Our diagnostic skills showed us where the learners are functioning. Our goal-setting skills showed us where the learners are going to learn to function. Now, our program development or programming skills are going to show us how to get there.

Our programming skills enable us to develop and implement the skill steps toward achieving our skill objective. Each skill objective is broken down to an atomistic level, beginning with our learners' levels of functioning. This way, we insure that our learners can achieve the skill objective. Most important, our programming skills enable us to tailor the learning programs to the learners' unique needs.

Facilitating Learner Action

Again, the learners know where they are beginning, where

PHASES OF LEARNING		TEACHING DELIVERY SKILLS	LEARNING PROCESS
	PRE-LEARNING	Preparing Content	
	1	Diagnosing	Exploring
	2	Goal Setting	Understanding
	3	Programming	Acting
	POST-LEARNING		

they are going and how to get there. They have every assurance that they will achieve their objective, due to the systematic development of their learning programs.

Thus, our programming skills facilitate the learners' essential movement through the action phase of learning: acting to get from where they are to where they want or need to be with the skills content. The learners can act to achieve their learning goals, and they can learn from the effectiveness of their actions how to modify future learning programs.

Framing The Program Around The Skill

The essential question of programming is: can we break down the steps to the skill objective so that the learners can perform them? The presentation is the primary phase when the teacher's programming skills are implemented. Our skill goals were set based upon our diagnoses of the learners' performances. When the learners can attend physically, then they can learn the observing and listening skills comprising the skill goal: attending to the learning experience.

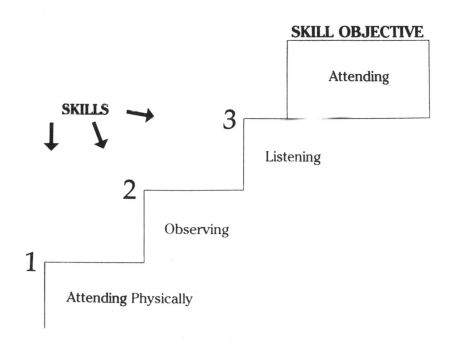

SKILL OBJECTIVE

Attending

SKILLS

3

Listening

2

Observing

1

Attending Physically

Generating The Skill Steps

After we have set the skills goals, then, we must develop the skills steps to achieve the goals. For example, in teaching attending physically as our learning skill goal, we have set an immediate objective of squaring, based upon our diagnosis of the learners' inability to square. Now we must treat the skill step of squaring as if it were a skill objective, and develop the subskill steps to achieve that objective.

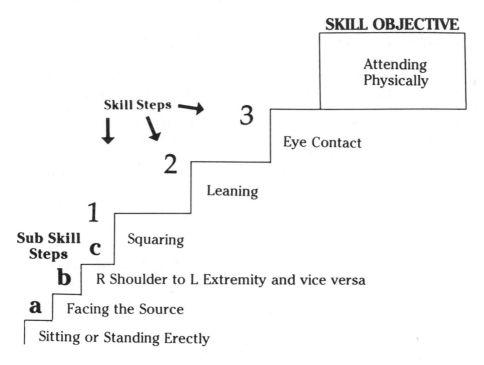

Integrating The Supportive Knowledge

Upon the development of the skill steps, we may discover that there are certain facts and/or concepts, in addition to the principle, that the learner lacks. For example, we have now introduced the concept of erectness, as well as other facts and concepts. Perhaps we have to define this with our how-after check steps: erectness is defined by the trunks of bodies being perpendicular to the level upon which we stand or sit. Thus, the learners will learn the supportive knowledge which they require to correctly perform the skill steps.

Designing A Sample Program

Our programming develops the skill steps and knowledge which the learners require in order to achieve the skill objective. Based upon the diagnosis of the learners' levels of functioning, the learning program provides all of the skills and knowledge required to achieve the skill objective. The learners have atomistic programs that lead them to their learning goals.

At this point, refer again to the skill objective for which you have developed your lesson plan. Develop the skill steps and knowledge for your learners based upon their unique objectives.

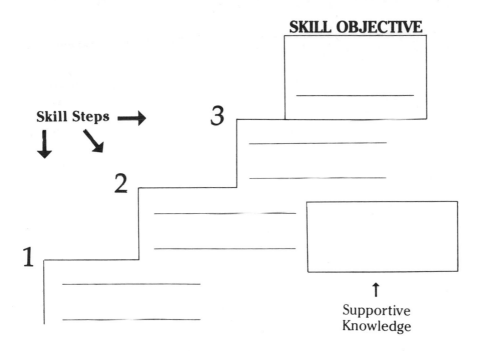

SKILL OBJECTIVE

Skill Steps →

3

2

1

↑
Supportive
Knowledge

Programming Is A Course of Action

Again, all content preparation is processed through the phases of learning. After using their goal-setting skills to facilitate the learners' understanding of where they want or need to be with the content, the teachers now use their programming skills to initiate action programs that will get the learners to the skill objective.

Programming, then, is the fourth step in delivery skills. It allows both teacher and learners to achieve the skills and knowledge objectives based upon the learners' diagnosis. In other words, the action programs are dependent upon both diagnosis and goal-setting. Both teacher and learners are now confident that they will get to where they are going.

MONITORING FOR EFFECTIVENESS

Monitoring Learner Performance

The purpose of the monitoring program is to observe the feedback from the learners' performances. Once the learners have acted on the program to achieve the learning objective, they receive feedback from their actions. The purpose of the monitoring is to assess this feedback.

The monitoring skills enable us to assess the applications the learners have made of the skills they have supposedly acquired. In other words, the monitoring skills assess the skills application in a real-life context. That, after all, is what the teaching and learning process is all about.

Recycling The Delivery Model

Our learners have acted upon their learning programs. They are attempting to apply the skills they have acquired. Monitoring skills will allow us to assess the effectiveness of this application. Accordingly, the exercise and summary phases will be the most effective times for the teacher to use the monitoring skills.

In so doing, our monitoring skills will serve to facilitate a recycling of learning. The learners have acted by attempting to perform the skill, and will now receive feedback from their actions. This feedback will serve to stimulate more extensive exploration of where the learners now are in relation to learning; thus, obtaining a more accurate understanding of where they now want or need to be; and therefore, determining more effective action to help them learn to perform the skill correctly.

PHASES OF LEARNING	TEACHING DELIVERY SKILLS	LEARNING PROCESS
PRE-LEARNING	Preparing Content	↓
1	Diagnosing →	Exploring
2	Goal Setting →	Understanding
3	Programming →	Acting
POST-LEARNING	Monitoring →	Recycling

Monitoring Skill Performance

The first application of monitoring is monitoring skill perfor-mance. The discrimination to be made here is simply whether or not the learners have applied the skills. If the skill has been performed, then the learner is giving evidence of readiness for the next learning experience. If the skill has not been performed, then the learner must recycle the learning experience.

For example, monitoring will determine whether or not the learner has performed the squaring skill as preparation for learning to attend physically to a learning experience. If the learner is squaring effectively, then the learner is ready to learn to lean, and then to make eye contact with the learning experience. If the learner is not squaring effectively, then the feedback stimulates a recycling of exploring where the learner is. For example, the learner may be able to sit erectly and face the source, but unable to place his or her right shoulder opposite the left extremity of the experience and vice versa. This recycling requires new goals to be set (right shoulder to left extremity and vice versa) and new programming to be done, in order to achieve this subgoal.

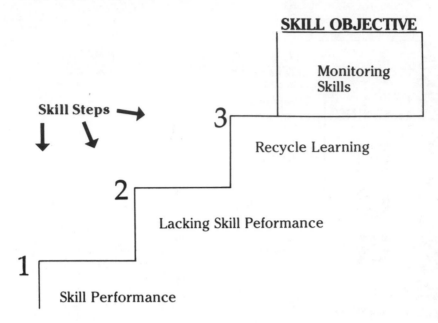

Discriminating Skill Steps

The second use of monitoring is when we apply this technique to the performance of skill steps. If the skill has not been performed,

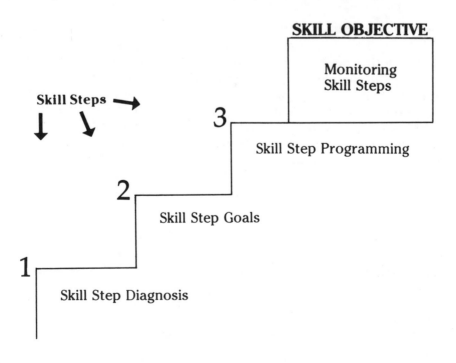

then the skill steps must be the learning process recycled.

For example, the learner may be able to sit erectly and face the source, but unable to place his or her right shoulder opposite the left extremity of the learning experience and vice versa. This new diagnosis facilitates the learner's new exploration of where he or she is with the skill. It requires a new goal to be set, i.e., right shoulder to left extremity, to facilitate the learner's more accurate understanding of where he or she wants or needs to be with the skill. A new program must be developed to initiate more effective action towards the achievement of this subgoal.

Checking The Supportive Knowledge

The third use of monitoring is checking the level of supportive knowledge available to the learner. If a skill step cannot be performed, then the supportive knowledge must be assessed in a recycling of the learning process.

For example, if the learner cannot bring himself or herself to face the learning experience and/or the teacher squarely, it may be because the learner lacks some level of supportive knowledge. Perhaps the learner comprehends the facts of the learning experience and teacher, and the concept of squaring.

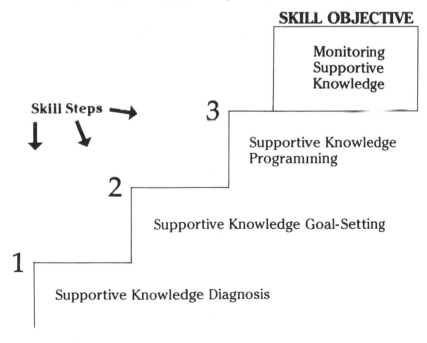

SKILL OBJECTIVE

Monitoring
Supportive
Knowledge

Skill Steps ⟶

3

Supportive Knowledge
Programming

2

Supportive Knowledge Goal-Setting

1

Supportive Knowledge Diagnosis

However, upon recycling, the learner may be diagnosed to lack comprehension of the principle of squaring: placing the right shoulder opposite the left extremity, and vice versa, enables the learner to observe the extremities of the learning experience and, thus, the entire experience. The knowledge of this principle becomes a goal, and a learning program is developed to achieve the goal.

Preparing To Monitor

Our monitoring skills enable us to assess the performance of skills and to recycle the learner into a new learning experience; or, to recycle the learner through select dimensions of the same or similar learning experience. If the learner fails to apply the skill correctly, then the learning process is recycled. The level of skill steps and supportive knowledge are diagnosed in order to help the learner to explore where he or she wants or needs to be. Programs are developed to help the learner get there.

At this point, use the skill objective for which you have developed your lesson plan again. Make certain you are prepared to monitor the skill application in order to determine whether to cycle the learner into a new learning experience, or recycle the learner through the same learning experience.

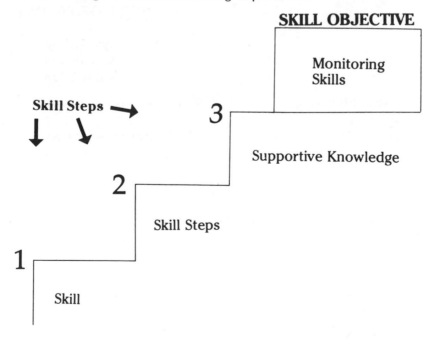

Monitoring The Application

Like the other teaching delivery skills, the monitoring skills serve to process the phases of learning. After the learners have acted to acquire the skills in the programming phase of delivery, the monitoring skills help us to assess the application of the skills in the postlearning phase. Depending upon the results of the assessment, the learner may be cycled through phases of a new learning experience, or recycled through phases of the previous learning experience. In the latter instance, monitoring serves to stimulate more extensive exploration, more accurate understanding, and more effective action on the part of the learners.

Monitoring, then, is the fifth step in delivery skills. It enables both teacher and learners to assess the effectiveness of the learners' skill applications. Thus, they have an objective basis for cycling or recycling learning. The monitoring skills assure the ongoing learning process that is necessary for student growth and development.

SUMMARIZING TEACHING DELIVERY

The Components Of The Delivery

Our expertise in our delivery skills is what enables us to develop teaching and learning programs. Because our content is developed and organized around skills, we are able to program every learner's experience. Each learner becomes a unique entity, with his or her own unique starting point for learning.

At this point, you may wish to consider, again, the delivery skills as you did initially. Where the preteaching assessment appeared difficult, it should now appear simple. You should be able to organize and sequence the delivery skills to meet learner needs for movement through the learning process.

Teaching Delivery Skills

Skill Steps: ___ ___ ___ ___ ___

Skill Objectives: ___ ___ ___ ___ ___

Principles: ___ ___ ___ ___ ___

Concepts: ___ ___ ___ ___ ___

Facts: ___ ___ ___ ___ ___

Your Delivery Skills

You may wish, again, to take a skill in your specialty content and outline how you would organize your teaching delivery now. Use the delivery skills which you have learned. Remember to process the content you have developed and organized through the learning process in which the learners engage. This time, reproduce the teaching system yourselves. That way you will get an index of how well you have learned your teaching delivery skills.

___ ___ ___ ___ ___

___ ___ ___ ___ ___

___ ___ ___ ___ ___

___ ___ ___ ___ ___

___ ___ ___ ___ ___

The Delivery System

We process our content through the phases of learning in order to individualize our learning programs. We prepare our content so that we can diagnose our learners. This facilitates the learners' exploration of where they are in relation to the content.

We individualize our goals based upon our diagnoses. This facilitates the learners' understanding of where they want or need to be with the content. We individualize our programs to achieve our goals. This facilitates the learners' action programs to get them from where they are to where they want to be with the content. We monitor the learners' skill performance. This cycles or recycles the learning process.

PHASES OF LEARNING		TEACHING DELIVERY SKILLS	LEARNING PROCESS
	PRE-LEARNING	Preparing Content	
	1	Diagnosing	Exploring
	2	Goal Setting	Understanding
	3	Programming	Acting
	POST-LEARNING	Monitoring	Recycling

A Human Delivery

Effective teachers teach learners, and we are effective teachers. We teach content to learners. Our teaching delivery is totally dependent upon moment-to-moment diagnosis of the learners' performance. We do not take still and static photos of living and learning. We take continuous and on-going motion pictures of the learner in interaction with the content.

These motion pictures enable every learner to succeed in every learning effort. Our learners cannot fail, because they begin where they are, and move to where they can go. They cannot fail because they are learning.

Our teaching delivery skills are based upon the moment-to-moment relationship of the learners with the content. They are also based upon the moment-to-moment relationship of the teacher with the learners. This is the topic of the next chapter.

RESEARCH BACKGROUND: TEACHING DELIVERY

The Principle of Teaching Delivery

The delivery of any set of skills and knowledge in any area of human endeavor requires both an external and an internal emphasis. The external frame of reference represents the skills content to be delivered. It is based upon the recipients' movement through the levels of these skills. At each step of skills development the recipient's progress is assessed. The helper, or teacher's skills utilization, is guided by the learners' movement toward the skill objective.

By and large, then, research has indicated that teachers are delivering their content in a manner facilitative of learning when they: (1) diagnose the learners in terms of their needs; (2) select and specify goals that are congruent with learner needs; (3) present the material in a highly cognitive and atomistic manner; and then (4) monitor the learning in terms of the goals that were specified. The basic principle of teaching delivery is that all effective teaching delivery is broken down in atomistic steps.

Research suggests that in delivering complex skills and knowledge, teachers should first assess the pupil's preinstructional functioning (diagnosis); then define the teaching goals, giving clear, positive instances along with indications of their critical characteristics (goal-setting); next, present the skills and knowledge, giving learners feedback after each response (programming); finally, continue to evaluate and provide feedback on the students' learning (monitoring) (Clark, 1971; Hudgins, 1974). All of these functions are incorporated in the teaching delivery skills.

The Dimensions of An Effective Delivery

In diagnosing where the learners are in relation to the content, it is important to gear the learning experience to the learners' needs. In addition, whether operating with high, moderate, or low ability in terms of the content, the learners will proceed to learn the same skills and knowledge, at their own individual paces. Caution should be exercised in limiting the learning tasks for low ability learners (Pfeiffer, 1966).

Learning goals should be based upon individual learners'

diagnoses. Specification of goals provide the learners with a clear understanding of where they want to be. Consequently, learners demonstrate greater interest, work involvement, self-direction and skills and knowledge achievements (Flanders, 1960, 1963).

A further increase in learner skills and knowledge is noted when the learning programs move in a highly cognitive and atomistic step-by-step manner. The learning program will move from the learner's level of functioning to the learning goal. The learners will have all of the steps they need to act to achieve the skill goal. (Flanders, 1965, 1966; Kaya, et al, 1967).

Again, monitoring should deal with precisely the same skills and knowledge which the learners have been taught. Too often, the teachers state one pattern of skills goals for the learners and then test and monitor another pattern of skills (Pfeiffer, 1966).

Summary of Research Findings

In summary, the teaching delivery skills (Chapter 5) maximize student involvement in the learning process (Berenson, Berenson and Carkhuff, 1978). The diagnosis facilitates the learners' exploration of where they are with the skills content. Goal-setting facilitates the learners' understanding of where they are in relation to where they want to be. Programming facilitates the learners' action to get to their skills goal. Monitoring facilitates the learners' recycling of the learning process. The teaching delivery skills offer a comprehensive approach to delivering content to learners.

In conclusion, the teaching delivery skills enable us to assess the learners' progress through the levels of the skills content. In so doing, we can be guided by what is effective in helping the learners to explore, understand and act upon their learning. We can maintain an external frame of reference representing objective reality.

References

Berenson, D. H., Berenson, Sarah R. and Carkhuff, R. R. *The Skills of Teaching - Lesson Planning Skills*. Amherst, Mass.: Human Resource Development Press, 1978.

Clark, D. C. "Teaching Concepts in the Classroom," *Journal of Educational Psychology* 62:253-278.

Flanders, N. A. "Diagnosing and Utilizing Social Structures in Classroom Learning," in *The Dynamics of Instructional Groups*, National Society for the Study of Education, 59th Yearbook, Part II. Chicago, Ill.: University of Chicago Press, 1960.

Flanders, N. A. "Teacher Influence in the Classroom: Research on Classroom Climate," in *Theory and Research in Teaching*, A. Bellack, ed. New York, N.Y.: Columbia Teacher's College, 1963.

Gage, N. L. *The Scientific Basis of the Art of Teaching*. New York, N.Y.: Teacher's College, 1977.

Hudgins, B. B. *Self-Contained Training Materials for Teacher Education*. Bloomington, Ind.: National Center for the Development of Training Materials in Teacher Education, Indiana University, 1974.

Kaya, E., Gerhard, M., Stasiewski, A. and Berenson, D. H. *Developing a Theory of Educational Practices for the Elementary School*. Norwalk, Conn.: Ford Foundation Fund for the Improvement of Education, 1967.

Pfeiffer, Isobel L. "Teaching in Ability-Grouped English Classes: A Study of Verbal Interaction and Cognitive Goals," *Journal of Teacher Education* 17: No. 3.

Interpersonal Skills 6

DEVELOPING EFFECTIVE INTERPERSONAL SKILLS

Your Teachers And You

Can we remember what our third grade reading teachers said after we recited our reading lessons? We may remember the names of all the different reading groups in which we participated, but it is difficult for most of us to recall what our teachers said.

Perhaps, then, we can remember what the teachers did not say. For sure, the teacher did not respond to our unique experience of learning: the happiness and satisfaction that came with a successful performance; the sadness and disappointment that came with a bad job; the anger and frustration that attended those words we never could get right – and still can't!

Perhaps we will recall what the teacher said when we read it and hear it again. The great majority of teachers for the great majority of times said, "Next!" Although it referred to the next learners and in that respect was related to their anxiety levels, this teaching response was totally unrelated to our unique learning experiences. As are nearly all of the responses we have heard – and made – over a lifetime!

The Interpersonal Principle of Learning

If we reflect upon our experiences as learners, we may feel sad about wasted opportunities, or we may even feel angry because we were cheated out of teacher responsiveness in developing our talents. Even today, there are learning situations which we cannot handle because of these earlier experiences.

As teachers, we feel disappointed because we have not been able to respond to our learners' unique experiences, though we would really like to. We really want to learn the interpersonal skills that will enable us to individualize the learners' learning programs.

The interpersonal principle of learning is most fundamental to the teaching-learning process: *all effective learning begins with the learners' frames of reference*. We must learn to enter the learners' frames of reference and relate our teaching delivery to the learners' experiences. The interpersonal skills that can be used to do this are the topics of this chapter.

Interpersonal Skills In The Delivery

Teachers are as effective as are their interpersonal skills. Ultimately, they implement the delivery of their content with their interpersonal skills. All other teaching skills may be functioning effectively, but if the teachers do not have high levels of interpersonal skills, they will fail to involve and move their learners in the learning experience.

Having developed and organized the content and methods, we teachers approach the delivery process. In facilitating the learners' movement through the phases of learning, we now use our interpersonal skills in conjunction with our delivery skills.

Now we are ready to relate our content and methods to our learners' experiences. We will do this through the use of our interpersonal skills. This is the moment of truth for teachers. For both teachers and learners it is an exciting and suspenseful time because nobody knows precisely how the relationship will turn out. It all depends upon how accurately the teachers perceive the learners' experience of learning.

A Survey Of Your Interpersonal Skills

We all understand the concept of relating to the learners' experience. We all use the term "empathy." The problem is that many times we do not understand the operations of this teaching skill. Just as with any content, it is difficult to define the skill objective and to develop the skill steps towards its achievement. Difficult, but not impossible!

Perhaps you can consider for a moment some of the interpersonal skills you employ. What do you call these interpersonal skills and what do they do? What are the principles that govern their effectiveness? How can they be defined as skills? How can you break out the skills steps to achieve the skills?

Skill Steps:	_____	_____	_____ _____
Skill Objectives:	_____	_____	_____ _____
Principles:	_____	_____	_____ _____
Concepts:	_____	_____	_____ _____
Facts:	_____	_____	_____ _____

At this point, it may be helpful to get an index of our previous learning about interpersonal skills. Perhaps you can take a skill in your specialty content and outline how you would employ inter-

PHASES OF LEARNING		TEACHING DELIVERY SKILLS	INTER-PERSONAL SKILLS	LEARNING PROCESS
	PRE-LEARNING	_____	_____	Involvement
		_____	_____	
	1	_____	_____	Exploring
		_____	_____	
	2	_____	_____	Understanding
		_____	_____	
	3	_____	_____	Acting
		_____	_____	
	POST-LEARNING	_____	_____	Recycling
		_____	_____	

personal skills to deliver it. In so doing, once again orient your interpersonal skills toward involving and moving the learners through the learning process.

The Dimensions Of Interpersonal Effectiveness

Clearly, there are many different interpersonal skills which we might list if we consider this area seriously.

Surely, the concept of empathy is paramount. The fact of relating one person's experience to another's through *responding* is supportive. The principle of reciprocal affect is relevant for the learners: they tend to relate to our experiences the way we relate to their experiences. The skill objective and skill steps are quite another thing. They are the topics of this lesson.

In addition to empathy, there are other concepts which we can develop. There is the concept of attentiveness or *attending* that makes *responding* to the experience of others possible.

As an extension of empathic *responsiveness*, there is the *personalized* response to the problems and goals of the learners.

A further extension of empathic responsiveness is found in the *individualized action programs* that the learners engage in to learn the skills necessary to achieve their *personalized* learning goals.

Finally, the culmination of empathic responsiveness is the individualized *reinforcement* of the learners' *action* to achieve the goals, which flows from and reflects the accurate empathic understanding of the teacher.

Can you define any or all of these interpersonal concepts as skill objectives and develop the skill steps to achieve them? Look at your outlines of your special contents and determine whether you developed operational steps for implementing your interpersonal skills.

The Interpersonal Skills

All of these interpersonal skills are illustrations of responses to the learners' experience. Together, they represent all of the skills the teacher needs to enter the learners' frames of reference and relate the content to the learners' personalized goals. These interpersonal teaching skills can be organized and sequenced for maximum facilitation of the learning process:

Attending to the learners, in order to **involve** them in learning.

Responding to the learners, in order to facilitate their **exploration** of the learning experience.

Personalizing the learners' experiences, in order to facilitate their **understanding** of themselves in relation to the learning experience.

Individualizing programs, to help the learners to **act** to get from where they are, to where they want to be with the learning experiences.

Reinforcing, in order to insure the learners' **action** and to consolidate skill gains.

ATTENDING TO THE LEARNERS

Being Attentive To The Learners

We prepare for our teaching delivery by attending to our learners. Attending means being attentive or paying attention to our learners, or simply that we care about what happens to them. So we poise ourselves to cover them with a "hovering attentiveness" just as we do with an infant.

When we provide our learners with our full and undivided attention, we are initiating the principle of reciprocal affect: the learners give us, in return, their full and undivided attention. The learners give us the input which we need to initiate the teaching delivery process.

Facilitating Learner Involvement

Attending involves the learners in the learning process. By attending to the learners we communicate an interest in their welfare. We also receive input and feedback concerning the effectiveness of the learning experience from the things we see and hear our learners do and say.

We attend to our learners in their absence when we develop and organize our content. We attend to our learners in their presence when we posture ourselves to attend physically to them, observe them, and listen to them. All of these attending skills serve to involve the learner in the learning process.

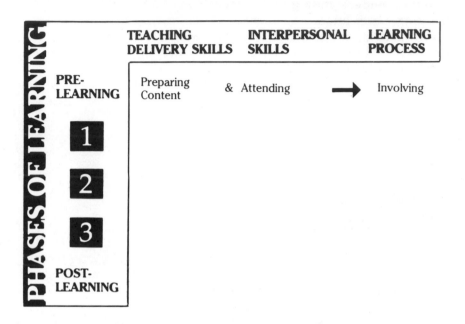

Attending Physically To The Learners

Attending physically means that we posture ourselves in such a way as to give our learners our full and undivided attention. It means that we are "with them." It is precisely this type of attention that we expect from our learners with regard to the learning experience.

As was covered in the initial stages of our learning skills program, we now use precisely the same skill steps that our learners employed. For example, in relation to our class or groups of learners, we position ourselves at the vertex of a right angle incorporating both extreme perimeters of the learners in our classroom. Similarly, we lean forward or toward our learners, just as we do with all things in which we are interested. Finally, we make frequent eye contact with all of our learners.

Practice these attending skills in groups of two or three. What other ways can you attend to your learners?

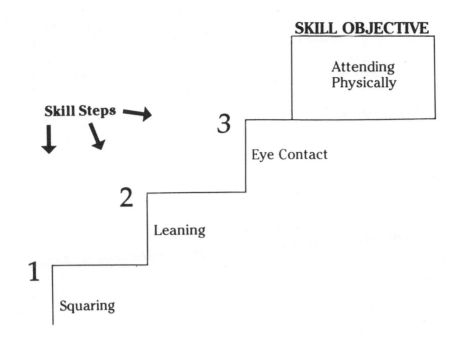

SKILL OBJECTIVE

Attending
Physically

Skill Steps →

3

Eye Contact

2

Leaning

1

Squaring

Observing The Learners

Observing means being able to "see" the appearance and behavior of learners, which give you clues to their experience: instead of a crowd of youthful faces, you see a frown, a grin, a pair of eyes that follow you in bright anticipation.

One way of observing both appearance and behavior is for us to watch the learners for exactly the same cues that we employ as teaching skills in attending physically. That is, we observe the learners' squaring, leaning and eyeing behavior.

We can make inferences from these cues. Physically, we can infer whether the learners have high, moderate or low levels of energy. Emotionally and interpersonally, we can infer whether they are "up," neutral or "down." Intellectually, we can infer whether they have a high, moderate or low level of readiness for learning.

Practice these observing skills in groups of two or three. What other dimensions can you observe in your learners?

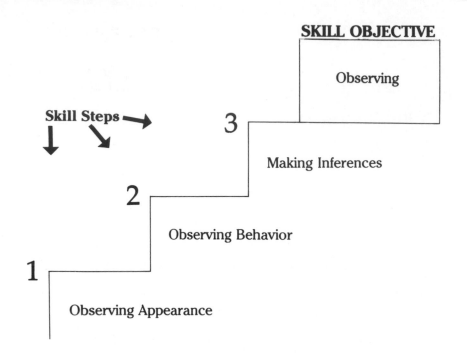

Listening To The Learners

Listening means being able to "hear" what has been said, and how it has been said, in order to understand the learners' experience. Instead of a babble of voices, we pick out this learner's calm and assured comment, or another's hesitant and embarrassed question.

The skill steps involved in listening include at least the following: suspending our own judgments, i.e., not listening to ourselves; resisting all distractions in order to focus upon the expression of the learners; and recalling the content of the learners' verbal expressions. These skill steps will insure that we have at least heard the content of the learners' expressions.

Practice repeating verbatim the content of the learners' expressions. What other dimensions are involved in listening?

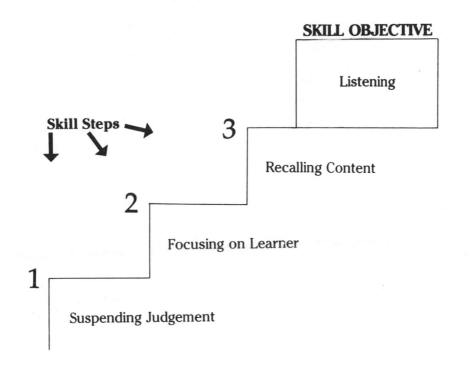

SKILL OBJECTIVE

Listening

Skill Steps →

3

Recalling Content

2

Focusing on Learner

1

Suspending Judgement

Using The Skills of Attending

Our attending skills involve at least three skill objectives: attending physically in order to pay attention to the learners; observing in order to "see" the learners; and listening, in order to "hear" the learners. In addition, attending physically prepares us for observing, and observing prepares us for listening. These attending skills, when employed simultaneously, will converge to involve the learners in the learning process.

At this point, you will want to practice using these skills simultaneously. First, practice attending physically, observing and listening with people, like yourselves, who are committed to learning teaching skills. Then apply these skills in your classrooms with your learners. You are sure to find the principle of reciprocal affect in operation: the learners will attend constructively to you to the same degree that you attend constructively to them.

Attending – The First Step In Interpersonal Skills

Attending, then, is the first step in our interpersonal skills development of the learning process. We attend to our learners in order to involve them in the learning process. Or, put another way, we attend to our learners so that they will attend to their learning experiences.

Attending skills set the stage for the teacher's response to the learners' experiences. First, when we signal to the learners that we are ready to give them our full and undivided attention they are more likely to start exploring themselves in relation to the learning experience. Second, attending skills serve to give us the cues we need to deliver our best responses, which, in turn, set the stage for making us effective teachers.

In summary, attending is a necessary but not sufficient condition of teaching. It involves the learners in the learning process. It tells us most of what we need to know about the learners. But it does not tell us what to do with what we know. Responding is the next step in our interpersonal skills learning program.

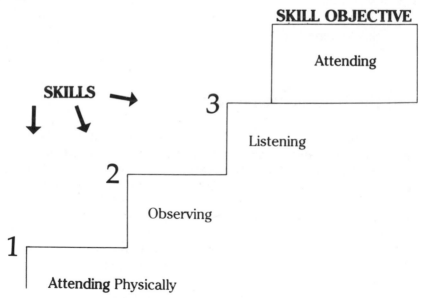

RESPONDING TO THE LEARNERS

Communicating Empathically

Responding is the key interpersonal ingredient. Responding means communicating an understanding of the experiences expressed by the learners. Responding means that we empathically enter the experiences of the learners – sit in their seats, see the experiences through their eyes – and communicate to them our understanding of those experiences.

When we respond to the learners' experiences we are accomplishing two essential teaching purposes: (1) we are coming into contact with the learners' frames of reference; and (2) we are bringing the learners into contact with their own frames of reference.

Again, the most fundamental principle of learning is that all learning begins with the learners' frames of reference. Our responsiveness is the way we enter the learners' experiences and communicate to them our understanding of their points of view.

Facilitating Learner Exploration

Responding initiates the first phase of learning. After involving the learners in the learning process through attending, we now facilitate their exploration through responding. Responding facili-

PHASES OF LEARNING		TEACHING DELIVERY SKILLS	INTERPERSONAL SKILLS	LEARNING PROCESS
	PRE-LEARNING	Preparing Content	& Attending	Involving
	1			
	2	Diagnosing	& Responding	Exploring
	3			
	POST-LEARNING			

tates the learners' exploration of where they are in relation to themselves, their teachers, the learning material or their worlds in general.

Responding skills are employed simultaneously with the diagnostic delivery skills to facilitate the learners' exploration. The responding skills serve to allow us to enter the learners' internal frames of reference. The diagnostic skills serve to assess the learners from an external – the teacher's – frame of reference. Both the responding and the diagnostic skills converge to facilitate the learners' exploration of where they are in the learning experience. It is clear to teacher and learners, from both an internal and external frame of reference, the point at which the learners begin their learning program.

Responding To Content

The first way of responding to our learners is to communicate our understanding of the content they are expressing. We can capture the content of an expression by repeating it verbatim. With more lengthy expressions, we can repeat the gist or the common theme.

For example, one of the learners might say the following:

"Those tests are always like that. They don't test what you know."

For responding to content, you can recall the content by repeating the expression verbatim to yourself. Then you can communicate your grasp of the content by reflecting the gist of it to the learners, using the reflective format, "You're saying _____."
For example, you might respond to the content in the above expression as follows:

"You're saying that the tests don't test what you know."

Practice capturing the common themes of learners in small training groups. Assign one person the role of teacher-trainer, another the role of teacher, and have the rest be learners. Then rotate the roles until each has had the opportunity to be the teacher. Have the teacher attempt to capture the gist of the content of the learners' expressions using the reflective format, "You're saying _____," or some other format that helps you to paraphrase the content.

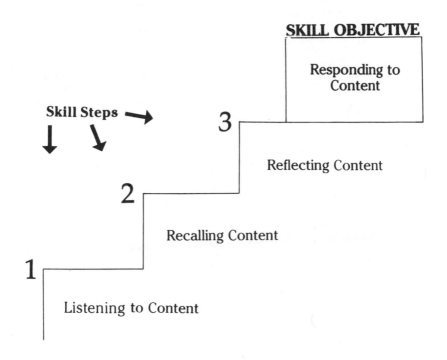

SKILL OBJECTIVE

Responding to
Content

Skill Steps ➡

3

Reflecting Content

2

Recalling Content

1

Listening to Content

Responding To Feeling

The second way of responding to our learners is to communicate our understanding of the learners' feelings about their experi-
taught to do so, and when they try they are often inaccurate and thus ineffective. They tend to introduce their own feelings prematurely and out of context. Thus, teachers say things like "you shouldn't feel that way," or "that's not the way it is," long before they have given the learners a chance to explore.

We can capture the feelings of an experience by doing three simple things: (1) repeating the expression verbatim to ourselves just as the learners expressed themselves to us; (2) asking ourselves, as if we were learners, "How does that make me feel?"; and (3) ences. Both teachers and learners are often reluctant to enter the realm of feelings. This is largely because teachers have not been using the reflective format for communicating the feeling, i.e., "You feel _____."

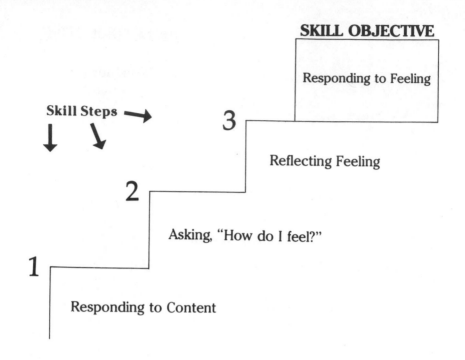

SKILL OBJECTIVE

Responding to Feeling

Skill Steps →

3

Reflecting Feeling

2

Asking, "How do I feel?"

1

Responding to Content

Expanding Feeling Words

For example, with the learners who stated that the tests didn't test what they knew, the teacher might respond as follows: "You feel upset."

One word of caution to teachers: often teachers do not use feeling words when they attempt to respond to their learners' experience. Following is the beginning of a list of basic categories of feelings at strong, mild and weak levels of intensity. Use your training groups to practice responding to feeling, and to expand your repertoires of feeling words for application in your classrooms.

Categories of Feelings

Levels of Intensity	Confused	Strong	Weak
Strong	Bewildered Trapped Troubled	Potent Super Powerful	Overwhelmed Impotent Small
	_____	_____	_____
	_____	_____	_____
Mild	Disorganized Mixed-Up Foggy	Energetic Confident Capable	Incapable Helpless Insecure
	_____	_____	_____
	_____	_____	_____
Weak	Bothered Uncomfortable Undecided	Sure Secure Durable	Shaky Unsure Soft
	_____	_____	_____
	_____	_____	_____

Levels of Intensity	Happy	Sad	Angry	Scared
Strong	Excited Elated Overjoyed	Hopeless Sorrowful Depressed	Furious Seething Enraged	Fearful Panicky Afraid
	_____	_____	_____	_____
	_____	_____	_____	_____
Mild	Cheerful Up Good	Upset Distressed Down	Annoyed Frustrated Agitated	Threatened Insecure Uneasy
	_____	_____	_____	_____
	_____	_____	_____	_____
Weak	Glad Content Satisfied	Sorry Lost Bad	Uptight Dismayed Put Out	Timid Unsure Nervous
	_____	_____	_____	_____
	_____	_____	_____	_____

Responding To Meaning

"Somehow", you may say, "the response to feeling seems incomplete."

"You're feeling confused because the response seems incomplete," is the response to make to such an expression.

Right on! The response to the learners' experience is incomplete without the meaning or the reason for the feeling. The response to feeling must be complemented by the reason for the feeling.

To develop our response to meaning we need only to: (1) build upon our feeling response; and (2) draw upon the content of the expression, asking ourselves the reason for the feeling. It remains only to use the reflective format to respond to the feeling and meaning, "You feel _____ because _____."

For example, we might formulate the following response to the learners who stated that tests didn't test what they knew: "You feel upset because the tests don't reflect what you know." This is a complete response to the learners' experience. It captures the feeling and the meaning.

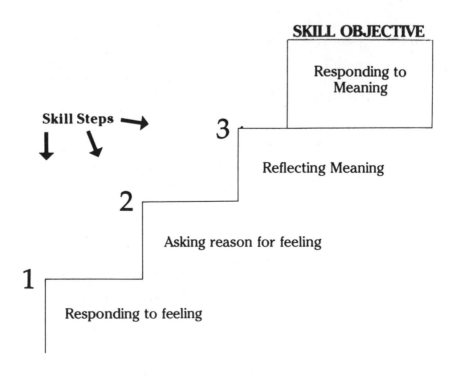

SKILL OBJECTIVE

Responding to Meaning

Skill Steps →

3

Reflecting Meaning

2

Asking reason for feeling

1

Responding to feeling

Practice responding to the feeling and meaning of learners' expression in small training groups, rotating the roles among trainer, teacher and learners.

Practicing The Skills of Responding

Our responding skills involve at least three skill objectives: responding to the content of the learners' expressions; responding to the feeling of the learners' experiences; and responding to the meaning of the learners' experiences. Each response prepares us for the next response. The responses to feeling and meaning culminate in our response to the learners' experiences. Responding accurately means that we are interchangeable in our understanding of the learners' frames of reference. By so doing, we have facilitated the learners' exploration of where they are in relation to their learning experiences.

While the review is the activity designed to gather input from the learners, our responding skills enable us to perform this diagnostic function in the moment-to-moment classroom interchanges that occur throughout the lesson.

At this point, you will want to practice using all of your responsive skills simultaneously. As is appropriate, you can respond to the content, feeling or meaning of the learners' experience. Practice these skills in training groups, then apply these skills in your classrooms.

Responding – The Second Step in Interpersonal Skills

Responding, then, is the second step in our interpersonal skills development of the learning process. We respond to our learners' experience in order to enter their frames of reference. We use our responding skills simultaneously with our diagnostic skills in order to facilitate the learners' exploration of where they are in relation to the learning experience.

Responding skills set the stage for personalizing the learners' experiences and individualizing the learners' goals. First, responding skills communicate our ability to assume their frames of reference.

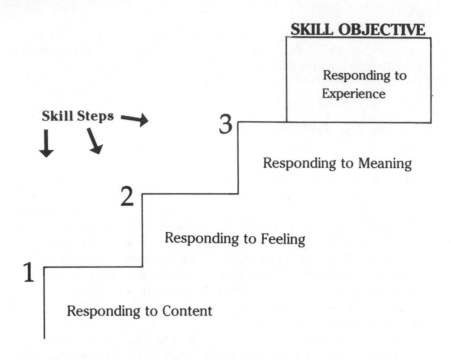

Second, they facilitate the learners' exploration of where they are within their own frames of reference.

In summary, responding is the key interpersonal skill for developing the learners' frames of reference: *the point where all learning begins.* This establishes a base for further movement into the learning process, towards personalizing the learners' understanding of where they are in relation to where they want or need to be. Personalizing is the next step in our interpersonal skills learning program.

PERSONALIZING THE LEARNERS' GOALS

Linking The Learners To The Learning

Personalizing provides the transition from exploration to

individualized action programs. Personalizing means individualizing the goals of learning. Personalizing means that we enter the learners' perceptions in order to develop goals that come from their frames of reference.

When we personalize the learners' understanding of their experience, we accomplish two essential teaching purposes: (1) we relate the learners' frames of reference to learning goals; and (2) we establish individualized goals that will guide the development of our individualized learning programs.

Our personalizing skills will enable us to extend the learners' frames of reference into goals that have value for the learners. Our personalizing skills will allow us to develop learning programs that will enable our learners to achieve their learning objectives.

Facilitating Learner Understanding

Personalizing introduces the second phase of learning. After responding to the learners' experiences in order to facilitate their exploration of where they are, we now personalize their understanding of their experiences. Personalizing helps the learners to understand where they are in relation to where they want or need

PHASES OF LEARNING		TEACHING DELIVERY SKILLS	INTERPERSONAL SKILLS	LEARNING PROCESS
	PRE-LEARNING	Preparing Content	& Attending	Involving
	1			
		Diagnosing	& Responding	Exploring
	2			
		Goal-Setting	& Personalizing	Understanding
	3			
	POST-LEARNING			

to be in their learning experiences.

Personalizing skills are used simultaneously with our goal-setting skills to facilitate the learners' understanding. The personalizing skills serve to extend the learners' internal frames of reference to an understanding of the externally derived goals. Both the personalizing and goal-setting skills converge to facilitate the learners' understanding of where they want or need to be in the learning experience. The goal of the learning program is therefore clear to teacher and learners from both an external, diagnostic frame of reference and also the learners' internal frames of reference.

Personalizing The Meaning

When we responded to the experience of the learners, we did so at the level the learners themselves expressed. We attempted to respond interchangeably with the feeling and meaning of their experiences. In so doing, we allowed the learners to externalize the meanings or the reasons for the feelings. We accepted the learners at the level they presented themselves. Now we are going to go beyond the learners' presentations.

We go beyond the learners' presentation by personalizing the meaning for the learners, through developing the implications of the experience for the learners. In so doing, we internalize the

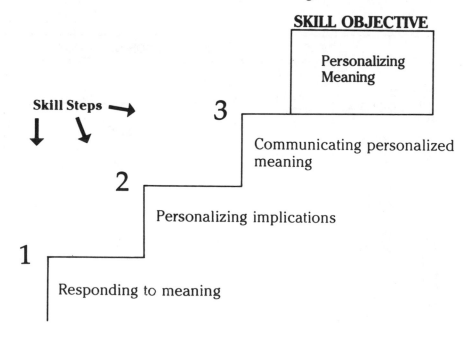

SKILL OBJECTIVE

Personalizing Meaning

Skill Steps ➝

3

Communicating personalized meaning

2

Personalizing implications

1

Responding to meaning

learners' responsibility for the experience.

For example, we responded to the meaning of the learner's experience when we said, "You feel upset because the tests don't reflect what you know." Now we ask a question concerning the personal implications for the learner: "What are the implications of the experience for me?" Foremost among the implications is the fact that the learner did not do well on the test.

It remains only to communicate this internalized meaning with the format: "You feel _____ because you _____." Thus, to continue this example, we may personalize our response to meaning as follows: "You feel upset because you didn't do well on the test."

Practice making personalized responses to meaning in small training groups, rotating the roles among trainer, teacher and learners.

Personalizing The Problem

Having personalized and internalized the meaning of the learner's experience, we now want to personalize the problem. After all, the learner's problem with the learning experience is an

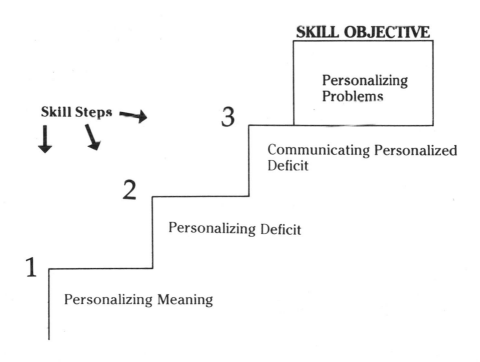

SKILL OBJECTIVE

Personalizing Problems

Skill Steps →

3

Communicating Personalized Deficit

2

Personalizing Deficit

1

Personalizing Meaning

obstacle to learning. We can personalize the problem by developing the learner's deficit in the learning experience. As if we were the learner, we ask the question, "What is it that I lack that led to this experience?"

For example, we personalized the meaning of the learner's experience with our response, "You feel upset because you didn't do well on the test." Now, we answer the deficit question for the learner: the learner lacks the ability to handle these tests effectively.

It remains for us to communicate this response deficit with the format: "You feel_____ because you cannot_____."
Thus, to continue the example, we may personalize the problem as follows: "You feel upset because you can't handle these tests." The response personalizes the problem for the learner.

Practice making personalized responses to problems in small training groups, rotating the roles among trainer, teacher and learners.

Personalizing The Feeling

After personalizing the problem, we must personalize the

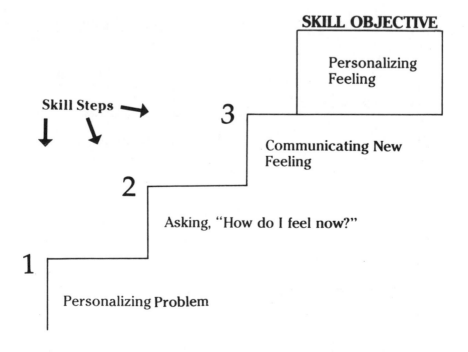

feeling. Our learner now has a different perception of the problem than he or she began with. The meaning has changed. For one thing, the learner has become accountable for his or her contribution to the experience. And so, the feeling may change. We personalize the feeling the same way that we responded to feeling. We ask the question, "How does that make me feel?", just as if we were the learner.

For example, we personalized the learner's problem when we said: "You feel upset because you cannot handle the tests." Now, we answer the new learning question for the learner. Does the learner feel upset? Or does the learner feel disappointed? All personalized feeling responses conclude in disappointment in oneself.

It remains for us to communicate this personalized feeling with the same format as the personalized problem: "You feel _____ because you cannot _____." Thus, to continue the example, we can personalize the feeling as follows: "You feel disappointed in yourself because you cannot handle these tests." The response personalizes the new feeling for the learner.

Practice making personalized feeling responses in small training groups, rotating the roles among trainer, teacher and learners.

Personalizing The Goal

Finally, we must personalize the goal. The problem, after all, dictates the goal. Indeed, the goal is simply the flip-side of the problem. The way we personalize the goal is simply to make explicit the goal that is implied by the personalized problem.

For example, we personalized the learner's problem and feeling when we said: "You feel disappointed in yourself because you cannot handle these tests." Now we simply append an explicit statement of the goal.

We do this by adding the goal statement: ". . . and you really want to." Thus, to continue our example, we may personalize the goal as follows: "You feel disappointed in yourself because you cannot handle these tests and you really want to." Such a response is a personalized goal statement.

Practice making personalized goal responses in small training groups, rotating the roles among trainer, teacher and learners.

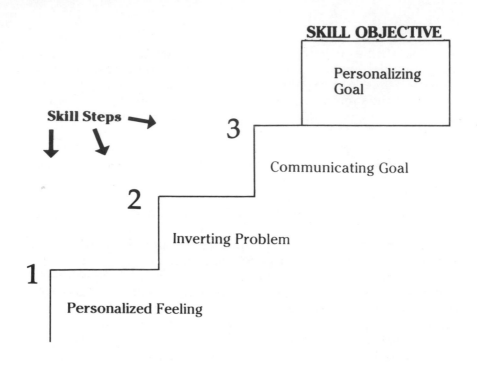

Using The Personalizing Skills

Our personalizing goal skills involve at least four skill objectives: personalizing meaning; personalizing problems; personalizing feelings; and personalizing goals. Each personalized response prepares us for the next response, just as responding to feeling and meaning prepared us for personalizing. By personalizing the learners' goals, we have gone beyond the learners' expressions. We have facilitated the learners' understanding of where they are in relation to where they want to be in the learning experience.

At this point, you will want to practice using our personalizing skills. Only now, unlike responding, you will use these skills sequentially. You will lay a base of responsive skills that are interchangeable with your learners' expressions. Then, you will move sequentially through your personalizing skills. You should always be careful to check your accuracy with your interchangeable responses to feeling and meaning. After you have practiced these skills in training groups, then you can apply them in your classrooms.

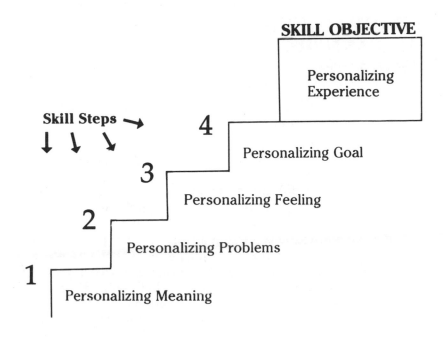

SKILL OBJECTIVE

Personalizing
Experience

Skill Steps →

4

Personalizing Goal

3

Personalizing Feeling

2

Personalizing Problems

1

Personalizing Meaning

Personalizing – The Third Step In Interpersonal Skills

Personalizing, then, is the third step in our interpersonal skills development of the learning process. We personalize our learners' experiences in order to add to their frames of reference. We use our personalizing skills simultaneously with our goal-setting skills, in order to facilitate the learners' understanding of where they want to be with the learning experience.

Personalizing skills set the stage for initiating individualized programs to achieve the learners' goals. First, personalizing skills communicate our ability to go beyond the learners' frames of reference to set learning goals. Second, they facilitate the learners' understanding of where they are in relation to where they want to be with the learning experience.

In summary, personalizing is the transitional interpersonal skill for developing learning goals: the point where learning concludes. This establishes a base for further movement into the learning process, to initiate in order to achieve the learning goals. Initiating is the next step in our interpersonal skills learning program.

INDIVIDUALIZING THE LEARNERS' PROGRAMS

Individualizing Learning

The learning process culminates in an individualized action program. Individualizing means tailoring the learning programs to meet the learners' unique needs. Individualizing means entering each learner's perceptions in order to relate each program to that individualized frame of reference.

When we individualize the learners' action programs, we accomplish two essential teaching purposes: (1) we relate the learners' frames of reference to the learning programs; and (2) we relate the learners' frames of reference to individualized reinforcements for achievement in the learning programs.

Our individualizing skills will enable us to help the learners to conclude the learning process. They will allow us to develop truly individualized learning programs that will enable our learners to achieve their learning objectives.

PHASES OF LEARNING		TEACHING DELIVERY SKILLS	INTERPERSONAL SKILLS	LEARNING PROCESS
	PRE-LEARNING	Preparing Content	& Attending	Involving
	1			
		Diagnosing	& Responding	Exploring
	2	Goal-Setting	& Personalizing	Understanding
	3	Programming	& Individualizing	Acting
	POST-LEARNING			

Facilitating Learner Action

Individualizing introduces the third phase of learning. Having personalized the learners' goals in order to facilitate their understanding of where they want or need to be, we now individualize their action programs to get there.

Individualizing skills are used simultaneously with our programming skills to facilitate the learners' action. The individualizing skills serve to extend the learners' internal frames of reference to relate to the externally derived action programs. Both the individualizing and programming skills converge to faciliate the learners' acting to get from where they are to where they want or need to be. The steps of the learning program are clear to teacher and learners from both our external, diagnostic frames of reference and the learners' internal frames of reference.

Developing Learning Principles

When we personalized the goal for the learners, we captured their skill disappointment in their response deficits and transformed their problems into goal statements. It remains for us to individualize the learning goals.

We individualize the learning goals by translating them into learning principles. Each learner can do this by developing an individualized learning principle that incorporates the skill to be learned, the particular application to be made and the unique human benefit to be achieved. To do this, we use the format for individualized learning principles: "If (*skill*), then (*application*) so that (*benefit*)."

For example, we personalized the learning goal for our learner: "You feel disappointed in yourself because you cannot handle these tests and you really want to." Now we will individualize the learning goal with an individualized learning principle: "If I learn test-taking skills (skill), then I will be able to handle these testing situations (application), so that I can learn the subjects I need to pursue the career I choose." Such a response is an individualized learning goal statement. By achieving the skill, the learner can make the unique application and receive the unique benefit.

Just as our responding skills operate to initiate the review or diagnostic functions in our classroom interactions, personalizing is a vehicle which enables us to set highly individualized goals. This may happen many times during the course of a lesson as opposed to the generalized objectives set during the overview and in goal setting delivery skills.

Practice making individualized learning goal statements in small training groups, rotating the roles among trainer, teacher and learners.

Framing The Diagnostic Skill Objectives

Having an individualized learning goal statement allows us to individualize the applications and benefits of learning. It also makes it possible to individualize the learning program. In much the same way as we are able to formulate personalized responses,

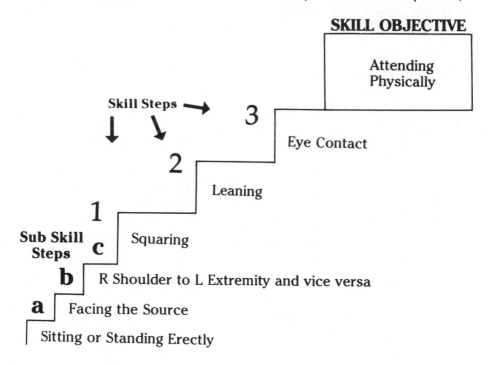

we can also personalize the learning program. Having seen, heard and responded to the learners' preference for or difficulty with methodology, we are able to individualize the content as well as the process the learners will use.

Remember, we have already developed our learning program from an external, diagnostic frame of reference with our teaching delivery programming skills. We have developed the skill steps to our attending physically skill objective. We have also developed the sub-steps to the first step of squaring.

For our individual learner, test-taking has been an area where the learner was deficient. In other words, the test-taking problem presented an obstacle to learning to attend physically.

Designing The Individualized Skill Objectives

Now we are going to individualize the learning program by developing the steps that come uniquely from the individual learner's internal·frame of reference. These steps will enable the learner to overcome the test-taking taking problem and achieve the first sub-step in the learning program.

We will develop the internalized learning program in the same manner that we developed the externalized program: by making the test-taking skills the skill objective and developing the steps and sub-steps to achieve it.

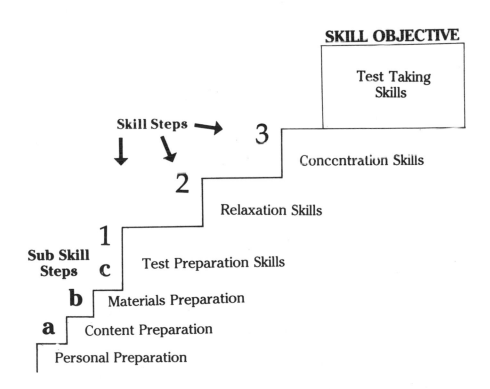

Programming For Individuals

Developing an individualized learning program is a matter of putting together the internalized and externalized skill steps. The internalized skills program leads from the individual learner's frame of reference to the first sub-step in the externalized skills program.

The internalized skills program overcomes the obstacle to learning (test-taking deficit) that prevented this particular learner from achieving the skill objective. By beginning from the learner's frame of reference, we are motivated instrumentally to achieve the skill objective by the knowledge of the application (handling testing situations) and the long-term personal benefits (pursuit of content and career).

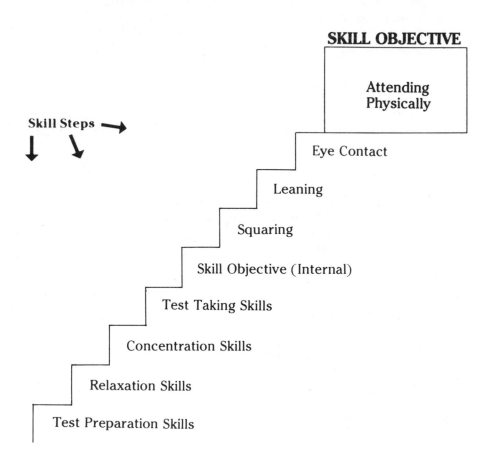

SKILL OBJECTIVE

Attending Physically

Skill Steps →

Eye Contact

Leaning

Squaring

Skill Objective (Internal)

Test Taking Skills

Concentration Skills

Relaxation Skills

Test Preparation Skills

Individualizing Learning Programs

Our individualizing program skills involve at least three skill objectives: developing individualized learning goals; developing skill steps from internal frames of reference; and developing individualized learning programs. Each individualized program prepares us for the next individualized program. By individualizing the learning programs, we have facilitated the learners' acting to get from where they really are, to where they need to be in order to get to where they want to be in their learning experiences.

At this point, you need to practice using your individualizing skills, individualizing: learning goals, internal skill steps, and learning programs. Be careful to relate the internal frame of reference of the learners to the external frame of reference of the subject content. After you have practiced these individualizing skills in training groups, then apply them in your classrooms.

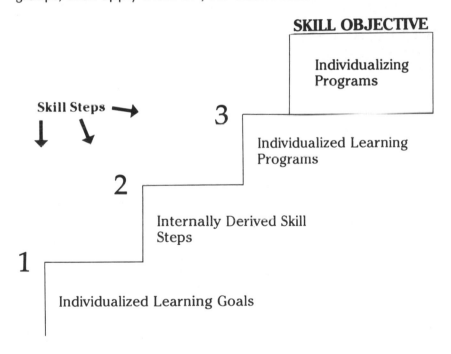

SKILL OBJECTIVE

Individualizing Programs

Skill Steps →

3

Individualized Learning Programs

2

Internally Derived Skill Steps

1

Individualized Learning Goals

Individualizing – The Fourth Step In Interpersonal Skills

Individualizing program skills, then, is the fourth step in our interpersonal skills development of the learning process. By individualizing the learning programs from the learners' frames of reference, we have made it possible for the learners to achieve learning goals in the external world of objective reality.

We have facilitated the learners' acting to get from where they are to where they want or need to be with externally determined, diagnostic learning goals. We have done this by facilitating the learners' acting with internally derived programs as were necessary to hook the learners up with the externally determined programs.

In summary, individualizing programs is the culminating act of the learning process. It involves all of the interpersonal skills we need to enter the learners' frames of reference and relate those perceptions programmatically to the learning goals. Individualizing programs is the fourth step in our interpersonal skills learning program. It remains for us to reinforce the individualized, programmatic learning.

REINFORCING THE LEARNERS

Individualizing Reinforcement

We have developed an individualized learning program. We did this by putting together programs drawn from the learner's internalized and the teacher's externalized frames of reference. It only remains to reinforce the achievement of each step in the learning program.

The reinforcement of learning flows directly from the learner's frame of reference just as did the individualized learning program. Indeed, the most potent reinforcement will be the long-term benefits that will accrue to the learner by learning the skills. The potency of the teacher's reinforcement is related directly to the empathy of the teacher for the learner.

Recycling Learning

Reinforcing serves to introduce the postlearning phase of recycling learning. Having individualized the learning programs to get the learners from where they are to where they want to be, we now individualize the reinforcements to get them there.

Reinforcing skills are used simultaneously with our monitoring skills to stimulate the recycling of learning. The reinforcing skills serve to strengthen the skills applications that are monitored. The reinforcing skills also enhance the skill steps and supportive knowledge needed to acquire and apply the skill. Together, the reinforcing and monitoring skills insure the correct application of the skill, requisite to the next cycle of learning.

PHASES OF LEARNING		TEACHING DELIVERY SKILLS	INTERPERSONAL SKILLS		LEARNING PROCESS
PRE-LEARNING		Preparing Content	& Attending	→	Involving
	1	Diagnosing	& Responding	→	Exploring
	2	Goal-Setting	& Personalizing	→	Understanding
	3	Programming	& Individualizing	→	Acting
POST-LEARNING		Monitoring	& Reinforcing	→	Recycling

Reinforcing Positively

The teacher uses his or her interpersonal skills to reinforce learning. The teacher simply makes a personalized response to learners' experiences based upon monitoring the skill application. In so doing, the teacher's task is to show the learners how learning each new skill, and making each new application, leads to the long-term benefit. Thus, the teacher personalizes the response by using the individualized learning principle:

"You feel _____ because you can (*skill application*) so that you are (*benefit*)."

Thus, for example, we might use the following positively reinforcing phrase with the learner in our illustration:

"You feel good because you are handling the tests so that you can move toward your career goals."

Such a response captures the feeling accompanying an effective skill application. It also complements the meaning of the skill application with the longterm benefit for the learner. This positively reinforcing response can also be used for the learning of skill steps and supportive knowledge, during either the cycling or recycling of learning.

Practice making positively reinforcing responses in small training groups, rotating the roles among trainer, teacher and learners.

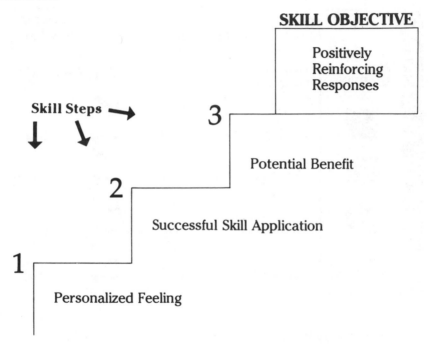

SKILL OBJECTIVE

Positively Reinforcing Responses

Skill Steps ➔

3

Potential Benefit

2

Successful Skill Application

1

Personalized Feeling

Reinforcing Negatively

Obviously not all skill applications are satisfactorily discharged by all learners. Clearly, the teacher must use interpersonal skills to make a personalized response to the problems the learners are encountering. As with positive reinforcements, the teacher will use the skill application and benefits to make negatively reinforcing responses:

"You feel _____ because you cannot (*skill application*) so that you are not (*benefit*)."

Thus, for example, we might use the following negatively reinforcing phrase with the learner in our illustration:

"You feel bad because you cannot handle the tests and you

are not moving toward your career goals."

Such a response captures the feeling and the problem of the learner's experience. At the same time, it does not punish the learner for his or her effort, however feeble. It puts the learning effort in the learner's hands by personalizing the response from the learner's frame of reference. This negatively reinforcing response can also be used for reinforcing learning skill steps and supportive knowledge.

Practice making negatively reinforcing responses in small training groups, rotating the roles among trainer, teacher and learners.

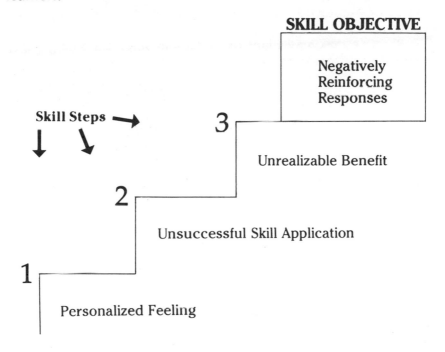

SKILL OBJECTIVE

Negatively
Reinforcing
Responses

Skill Steps →

3

Unrealizable Benefit

2

Unsuccessful Skill Application

1

Personalized Feeling

Being Vigilant

Finally, it is sometimes unclear to the teacher whether or not the learners are making effective skill applications. This is usually because the learner is not clear. It may require intense vigilance and fine discrimination on the teacher's part to make the determination. Ultimately, it must be determined before the learner moves on to new learning: either the learner has made the skill application or not. Accordingly, the teacher will either make a positively or negatively reinforcing response. In any event, the teacher can use interpersonal skills to respond to the learner's experience at the moment:

"You feel _____ because sometimes you can and sometimes you cannot (*skill application*) so that you are not clear about (*benefits*)."

Thus, in the illustration, we might respond to the learner's mixed experience:

"You feel confused because you are handling some testing situations and not others, so that you are not clear about your movement toward your career goals."

Such a response comes from the learner's frame of reference, yet allows the teacher time to observe the learner's performance. It can also be employed for the learning of skill steps and supportive knowledge.

Practice making vigilant responses in small training groups, rotating the different participants in different roles.

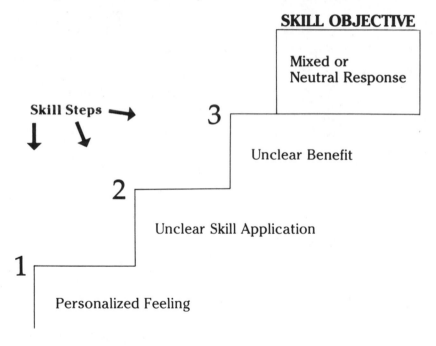

Practicing Reinforcing Tasks

Our individualized reinforcing skills involve at least three skill objectives: positively reinforcing responses; negatively reinforcing responses; and mixed or neutral responses. Each reinforcing response comes from the learner's own unique frame of reference. It incorporates the learner's feeling experience, skill application and benefit.

At this point, practice using your reinforcing skills. Always emphasize observing the learner's performance vigilantly, in order to determine whether it is moving him or her toward or away from the skill application and the human benefit. After you have practiced these reinforcing skills in training groups, then you will want to apply them in your classrooms.

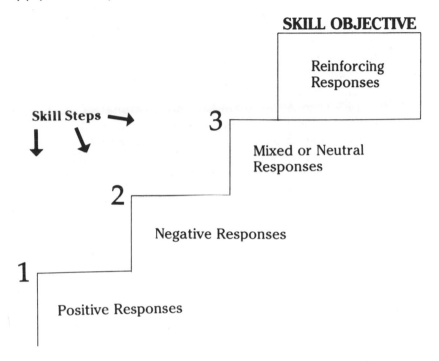

SKILL OBJECTIVE

Reinforcing Responses

Skill Steps →

3

Mixed or Neutral Responses

2

Negative Responses

1

Positive Responses

Reinforcing – The Fifth Step in Interpersonal Skills

Reinforcing responses allow us to strengthen the skillful applications (positive), weaken the unskilled applications (negative) and extinguish the unclear applications (mixed or neutral). Thus, reinforcing responses make it possible for our learners to move on in their learning programs.

In summary, reinforcing responses serve to stimulate the cycling or recycling of learning, depending upon the monitoring of skill applications. These responses involve all of the interpersonal skills we have to relate learner experience to learner performance. The quality of empathy and reinforcements are directly related. Reinforcing responses is the final step in our interpersonal skills learning program.

SUMMARIZING THE INTERPERSONAL SKILLS

Organizing The Interpersonal Dimensions

Our expertise in interpersonal skills is what enables us to individualize learning programs. We have used our programming skills to develop our learning programs. Now we can use our interpersonal skills to individualize the learning programs to meet the learners' unique perceptions.

At this point, consider again the interpersonal skills, as you initially did. Whereas it may have previously been difficult to define dimensions such as empathy, you should now be able to break out all of the interpersonal dimensions. You should be able to organize and sequence the interpersonal skills to meet learner needs for movement through the learning process.

Interpersonal Skills

Skill Steps:	___	___	___	___	___
Skill Objectives:	___	___	___	___	___
Principles:	___	___	___	___	___
Concepts:	___	___	___	___	___
Facts:	___	___	___	___	___

Looking Over Your Interpersonal Skills

Take a skill in your specialty content and outline how you would organize your interpersonal skills now. Use your interpersonal skills in conjunction with the delivery skills you have learned. Sequence them in relation to the phases of learning in which the learners engage. This time, reproduce the teaching system yourselves. That way you will get an index of how well you have learned your interpersonal skills.

Reviewing The Interpersonal Model

As can be seen, we attend to our learners in order to involve them in the learning process. We respond to our learners in order to individualize our diagnoses and facilitate the learners' exploration of where they are in relation to the learning experience. We personalize our responses in order to individualize our goals and facilitate the learners' understanding of where they want or need to be in the learning experience. We individualize our responses in order to individualize our programs and facilitate the learners' acting to get from where they are to where they want to be with the learning experience.

PHASES OF LEARNING		TEACHING DELIVERY SKILLS	INTERPERSONAL SKILLS	LEARNING PROCESS
PRE-LEARNING		Preparing Content	& Attending	Involving
	1	Diagnosing	& Responding	Exploring
	2	Goal-Setting	& Personalizing	Understanding
	3	Programming	& Individualizing	Acting
POST-LEARNING		Monitoring	& Reinforcing	Recycling

Individualizing A Human Delivery

Yes, effective teachers teach learners. They individualize the learning programs so that the learners find themselves within the programs. Just as the learning program is dependent upon a moment-to-moment diagnosis of external performance, so is the individualized learning program dependent upon a moment-to-moment empathy with internal experience. We need to develop as many momentary internal and external programs as are necessary to insure the learning delivery.

Our interpersonal skills enable us to become fully human beings, to enter our homes and our schools with the confidence that we can share another human being's experience. Most important, our interpersonal skills enable us to relate our experiences to other's without violating the integrity of either. Indeed, they allow us to develop individualized programs of growth for both teacher and learners.

Our interpersonal skills, used in conjunction with our teaching delivery skills, enable us to stay tuned to the internal experiences of the learners and the objective reality of the curriculum. They put the human being into the human learning equation. We are eager to get started with our real-life applications.

RESEARCH BACKGROUND: INTERPERSONAL SKILLS

The Substance of Human Relations

Perhaps the most important set of skills that any one human being can have is the ability to relate to another human being. The active ingredients that serve to facilitate or retard human relationships and human resource development are interpersonal. Depending upon the level of concession by the "less knowing" person, the "more knowing" person may have dramatically constructive or destructive human effects, or any degrees in between these extremes.

Interpersonal skills are the substance of human relations. These skills enable a person to walk, as the Indians say, in another person's mocassins; to see the world through another's eyes and communicate what is seen; to assist another person in surmounting problems and achieving goals.

Interpersonal skills emphasize the internal frame of reference of the learner/recipients, based upon the learner's experience of movement through the levels of the skill content. Most fundamentally, these skills enable the teacher to relate the learners' frames of reference to the teaching goals. They are the catalysts that activate the learners to receive all other teaching ingredients.

The Principle of Interpersonal Effectiveness

A number of studies have shown that the teachers' interpersonal skills relate to the learners' academic, as well as social, achievement. In particular, these interpersonal skills can be summarized as attending or paying attention; responding or being empathic; personalizing or being additive in understanding the learners' problems and goals; individualizing or initiating programs to meet the learners' unique needs; and reinforcing the learners from their own internal frames of reference. The basic principle of interpersonal skills being that all effective learning begins with the learners' frames of reference.

Attending directs the teacher's attention to the learners. The teacher observes and listens to the learners with a kind of "hovering attentiveness." In turn, the learners tend to return this attention via the principle of reciprocal affect (Carkhuff, 1977). Attending is a necessary but not sufficient condition of responding.

Responding relates to the teachers' efforts to empathize with the learners. There are at least two sets of skills involved here: discriminating the learners' experiences; and communicating the learners' experiences. A great deal of research has been mounted in support of the teachers' ability to communicate empathic understanding and the learners' achievement (Aspy, 1972; Aspy and Roebuck, 1977; Bloom, et al, 1956; Carkhuff, 1969, 1971; Flanders, 1970).

Personalizing is an extension of responding. Personalizing serves simply to help the learners to internalize responsibility for learning problems and, thus, for achieving learning goals. Personalizing specifies the personal goals to be achieved through individualized programs (Carkhuff, 1977).

Individualizing refers to the process of moving programmatically from the learners' internal frames of reference to the learners' externally based learning programs. This process makes truly individualized learning programs possible (Carkhuff, 1977).

Reinforcing flows directly from personalized responding. Reinforcements are effective only if derived from the learners' frames of reference. There is a great deal of evidence to indicate that positive reinforcements, such as praise and punishments, such as criticism or disapproval, when used sparingly, are related to learner achievement (Gage, 1977).

Summary of Research Findings

In summary, interpersonal skills (Chapter 6) serve to engage the learners in the learning process (Carkhuff, Berenson and Pierce, 1976): attending facilitates involvement; responding facilitates exploration; personalizing facilitates understanding; individualizing initiates action; and reinforcing recycles learning. Interpersonal skills offer a comprehensive approach to relating teachers to the students' frames of reference.

In conclusion, interpersonal skills enable us to assess the learner/recipients' progress through the eyes of the learners themselves. In so doing, we can relate the learners' internal frames of reference to the external frame of the skills content. Thus, we can be guided by what is effective in helping the learners to move through the phases of learning. Our interpersonal skills enable us to converge objective reality with subjective experience.

References

Aspy, D. N. *Toward a Technology for Humanizing Education.* Champaign, Ill.: Research Press, 1972.

Aspy, D. N. and Roebuck, Flora N. *KIDS Don't Learn from People They Don't Like.* Amherst, Mass.: Human Resource Development Press, 1977.

Bloom, B. S., Englehart, M. D., Furst, E. J., Hill, W. H. and Kratwohl, D. R. *A Taxonomy of Educational Objectives: Handbook I, The Cognitive Domain.* New York, N.Y.: Longmans, Green, 1956.

Carkhuff, R. R. *Helping and Human Relations.* New York, N.Y.: Holt, Rinehart & Winston, 1969.

Carkhuff, R. R. *The Development of Human Resources.* New York, N.Y.: Holt, Rinehart & Winston, 1971.

Carkhuff, R. R. *The Art of Helping.* Amherst, Mass.: Human Resource Development Press, 1977.

Carkhuff, R. R., Berenson, D. H. and Pierce, R. M. *The Skills of Teaching Interpersonal Skills.* Amherst, Mass.: Human Resource Development Press, 1977.

Flanders, N. A. *Analyzing Teaching Behavior.* Reading, Mass.: Addison-Wesley, 1970.

Gage, N. L. *The Scientific Basis of the Art of Teaching.* New York, N.Y.: Teachers College Press, 1977.

The
Teaching System   7

A SUMMARY
OF SKILLS

Sources of Teaching Effectiveness

When the teacher closes the door in the classroom, there are only three sources of teaching effectiveness: the teacher, the learners and the content. However supportive other teachers, or administrators, or parents may be, the individual teachers are on their own. However successful the teachers have been with past students, this is a new group of learners. However many stacks of curricula exist in the desks or on the shelves, the teachers must think and act on their feet. That total dependency upon self is what makes teaching so exciting and so demanding at the same time.

This is really what the skills of teaching are all about – thinking and acting on our feet, to meet the needs of learners at the moment. Developing a principle! Reviewing a contingency skill! Filling in a missing show step! Diagnosing performance! Individualizing a learning program! These are generic skills that we can stick in our hip pockets, enabling us to teach effectively at any moment!

Teaching Skills – Summarizing Your Learning

Before we extend our conclusions any further, once again you should get an index of your ability to achieve your goals in teaching. Simply outline the teaching skills that you would employ to accomplish your teaching goals. Outline the skills as you now understand them to relate to the following sources:

Teacher: _____

_____

_____

_____

Learner: _____

_____

_____

_____

Content: _____

_____

_____

_____

At this point you may also want to develop your specialty content. That way, you can compare your current programs with the programs which you produced at the beginning of this teaching. This will give you a check on your overall level of learning over the course of the skills of teaching program.

THE TEACHER AS INSTRUCTIONAL LEADER

The TLC System – A Teacher-based System

Hopefully, you will recognize the growth of your skills in

teaching. Over the course of your learning you should have acquired the facts, concepts and principles of teaching skills and applied the skills in your classrooms. You should be able to see the difference not only in what you *know* now, but also in what you can *do* now.

You should by now realize that the TLC System – teacher, learners, content – is a teacher-based one. The content can do nothing on its own until the teacher has developed and organized it. The learners can do nothing on their own until the teachers have taught them what to do.

The effectiveness of teaching is based upon the skills of teachers. The skillful teachers make the learners and the content effective sources of learning. The generic skills that the teachers possess are what mobilize and energize the learning that takes place in the classroom.

Teacher As Developer – Skills-Based Curricula

The essential beginning point of our teaching skills is our content development skills. These skills allow us to take any *facts* and *concepts* in our different curricula and develop them into *principles*. Often, these principles are not available in our books and materials. With these principles, we can develop *skill objectives* and the *skill steps* to achieve the skill objectives.

Content development skills yield enormous power for transforming any concept into skills. In the hands of a skillful teacher, the skills content may be transmitted effectively to any group of learners. Since this is the summary, see if you can *tell-show-do*, transforming one of the concepts of your content into a skill objective and the skill steps to achieve it.

Levels of Content

Skills	Skill Steps: _____	
	Skill objectives: _____	
Knowledge	Principles: _____	
	Concepts: _____	
	Facts: _____	

Teacher As Planner – Application-Based Lesson Plans

One of the sets of skills for transmitting content efficiently and effectively to learners is lesson-planning skills. Lesson-planning skills enable us to organize our content around the skills application. In other words, the application of the skills is the purpose for learning the skill steps. The skills and supportive knowledge of our content are funnelled into the phases of content organization: *reviewing; overviewing; presenting; exercising;* and *summarizing.*

Lesson planning skills facilitate the transformation of skill steps into skill applications. In the hands of a skillful teacher, the skills content can be transmitted efficiently to any group of learners.

CONTENT ORGANIZATION	CONTENT SKILLS		KNOWLEDGE
	Skill Steps	Skill Objective	Principles Concepts Facts
REVIEW	Contingency Skills	&	Supportive Knowledge
OVERVIEW	Skill Application	&	Supportive Knowledge
PRESENT	Skill Steps	&	Supportive Knowledge
EXERCISE	Skill Steps	&	Supportive Knowledge
SUMMARIZE	Skill Steps	&	Supportive Knowledge

Teacher As Manager – Learning-Based Teaching Methods

Another set of skills for transmitting content experientially to learners is teaching methods. Teaching methods enable us to organize our content delivery around the learners' kinesthetic learning experiences. In other words, the outcome of the use of our teaching methods is the direct involvement of our learners in acquiring, applying and transferring skills. The teachers *tell* and *show* so that the learners will learn to *tell, show* and *do*.

As can be seen, much of the teacher's classroom time is spent managing learning. The review, exercise and summary emphasize managing the learners' *tell-show-do* activities. The overview involves the teacher's comparison of his or her image, and the management of the development of the learners' images of the *tell-show-do* activities. The presentation emphasizes the teacher's *tell* and *show* and the management of the learners' *do* activities.

Teaching methods facilitate the learners' application of skills through the use of the didactic, modeling and experiential sources of learning. In the hands of a skillful teacher, the skills content can be transmitted experientially to any group of learners. As a summary, see if you can *tell-show-do* the application of the skill steps of your content.

	Content Level	Teaching Methods	Teacher as Manager
R	Contingency Skills	Tell, Show, Do	**Managing Learning**
O	Skill Application	Tell, Show, Do	**Overviewing Managing Learning**
P	Skill Steps	Tell, Show, Do	**Presenting Managing Learning**
E	Skill Steps	Tell, Show, Do, Repeat, Apply	**Managing Learning**
S	Skill Steps	Tell, Show, Do, Repeat, Apply	**Managing Learning**

(CONTENT ORGANIZATION)

Teacher As Programmer – Programmatic Deliveries

With the skills content prepared, the teacher is ready to enter into a delivery mode with the learners. The skills content, organized in a lesson plan, is funnelled into the prelearning phase of learning. In other words, the content is prepared before the teacher enters a delivery relationship with the learners. With the content prepared, the teacher then diagnoses, sets goals, programs and monitors the learning.

Teaching delivery skills operationalize the atomistic steps required by the learners to achieve their skill objectives. In the hands of a skillful teacher, the skills content may be delivered directly to any group of learners.

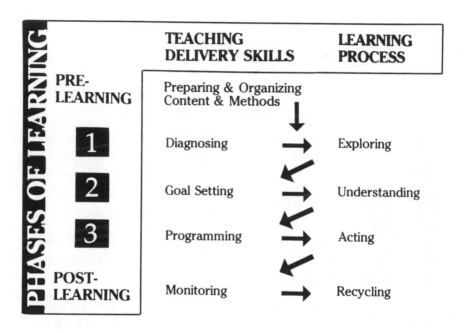

Teacher As Helper – Individualized Learning Programs

The teacher employs interpersonal skills in conjunction with the teaching delivery skills to individualize the learning programs. By *attending* and *responding* and *personalizing* the learner's experience, the teacher is able to bridge the gap from the learner's internal frame of reference to the external, diagnostic frame of reference based upon the skills content. Because the teacher is able to enter the perceptions of the learner, the teacher is able to relate that frame of reference to the teaching goals. The teacher is able to *individualize* and *reinforce* the learning program.

Interpersonal skills, then, relate the learners' frames of reference to the skills content. In the hands of a skillful learner, the skills content will be modified in an individualized learning program.

PHASES OF LEARNING		TEACHING DELIVERY SKILLS	INTERPERSONAL SKILLS	LEARNING PROCESS
	PRE-LEARNING	Preparing Content	& Attending	Involving
1		Diagnosing	& Responding	Exploring
2		Goal-Setting	& Personalizing	Understanding
3		Programming	& Individualizing	Acting
	POST-LEARNING	Monitoring	& Reinforcing	Recycling

The Skilled Teacher-The Whole Teacher

A good summary will be for you to recognize the degree to which we employed teaching skills in our own teaching skills program. If you reflect upon the development of **The Skilled Teacher**, you will recognize the internal consistency of this teaching. As a summary exercise, you might want to go back through the book and identify these teaching ingredients. Here is what you will find:

Our content was developed in *skill objectives* and *skill steps* with the necessary *supporting knowledge*.

Our lesson plans organized the content to *review* contingency skills, to *overview* skill applications and to *present, exercise* and *summarize* skill steps.

Our teaching methods emphasized didactic (*tell*), modeling (*show*) and experiential (*do*) sources of learning.

Our teaching delivery skills enabled us to *diagnose, set goals, program* and *monitor* the learning, to the degree possible.

Our interpersonal skills allowed us to *attend, respond, personalize, individualize* and *reinforce* our learning programs, to the degree possible.

Right now, we have a sense of completeness – of fullness, a sense of excitement and anticipation of the future – because we *know* something and can *do* something that we could not do before learning teaching skills. It remains for us to practice these skills in our classrooms and, even more importantly, in our daily lives.

TEACHER AS LEARNING SYSTEM MANAGER

The Responsibilities of Teaching

Thus, we can see that a teacher is more than a teacher. The functions within the teaching triangle show us this. A teacher is a *developer*, a *planner*, a *manager*, a *programmer* and a *helper*. These are the primary functions of a teacher.

Nowhere else are there more functions. In no other career are there more responsibilities. In no other way of life is the growth and development of more people dependent upon the skills of one person.

As teachers, we, above all others, have the responsibility for developing the skills of our youth. Their ability to actualize the potential of their generation is dependent upon our ability to actualize our teaching potential. This responsibility is discharged with our teaching skills alone, and our ability to use these teaching skills to develop new teaching and learning programs.

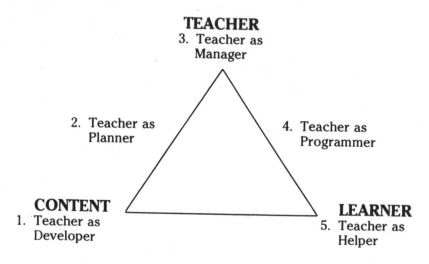

The Principles of Teaching

As teachers, we become our own technology developers. Because we have the generic skills, we are able to develop our own skills-based learning programs based upon the fundamental principles of teaching and learning.

As a content developer, the teacher is implementing the basic principle of content development: *all effective content culminates in a skill objective.*

As a planner, the teacher is implementing the basic principle of lesson planning: *all effective lesson plans are organized around a skill application.*

As a manager of learning, the teacher is implementing the basic principle of teaching methods: *all effective teaching methods emphasize kinesthetic learning.*

As a programmer of learning, the teacher is implementing the basic principle of teaching delivery: *all effective teaching is broken down into atomistic steps.*

Finally, as a helper, the teacher is implementing the basic principle of interpersonal skills delivery: *all learning begins with the learner's frame of reference.*

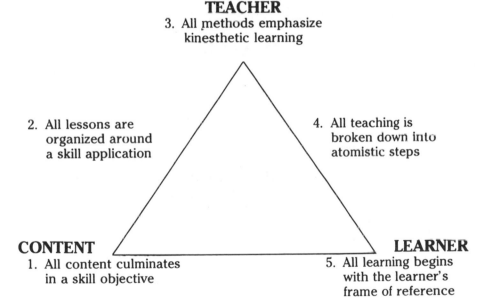

TEACHER
3. All methods emphasize kinesthetic learning

2. All lessons are organized around a skill application

4. All teaching is broken down into atomistic steps

CONTENT
1. All content culminates in a skill objective

LEARNER
5. All learning begins with the learner's frame of reference

Learning Management Skills

Thus far, we have focused upon a teacher-based system. While the teacher relates to the learners through the content, the ultimate purpose is to relate the learners to the content. Indeed, the learner/products of our teaching programs need to be equipped to manage their own learning throughout their lives.

One way of developing this expertise in learners is to teach them learning management skills. In other words, we teach them how to manage the reception of the skills we are delivering. For every set of teaching skills there is a learning management counterpart.

Thus, for example, we know what explorations to make and actions to take concerning the skills or knowledge to be learned (*content development*); the stages of content organization to process (*lesson planning*); the *tell-show-do* teacher and learner functions (*teaching methods*); the programming delivery process (*teaching delivery*); and the individualizing delivery process (*interpersonal skills*).

In the end, how the learners are able to acquire, apply and transfer the content will be the measure of the effectiveness of our teaching. Indeed, how the learners manage their own learning will be the measure of their ability to be involved in life-long growth.

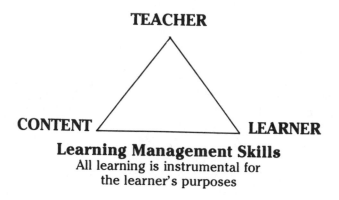

TEACHER

CONTENT   **LEARNER**

Learning Management Skills
All learning is instrumental for
the learner's purposes

Administrator Support Skills

In addition, the teacher needs every bit of assistance possible inside of the school. In order to make this possible, the teachers and the administrators must not be working at cross purposes. The teachers must make the administrators aware of the skills the teachers are employing, and the activities in which the learners are engaging.

This means the teachers must treat the administrators as learners, involving them in a growth process. It also means the teachers must treat the administrators as teachers, receiving their input and feedback concerning the teaching skills programs.

Most important, the teachers must help the administrators to develop the discrimination skills which they require to perform their administrative functions of planning, managing, monitoring, evaluating and reinforcing the teaching and learning programs. These topics will be considered in depth in another work on "Administrator Support Skills."

In conclusion, how well we can "school" our own administrators in the skills and knowledge involved in the administration of our teaching and learning programs, will determine how much real assistance they provide in our development and the development of our learner/products.

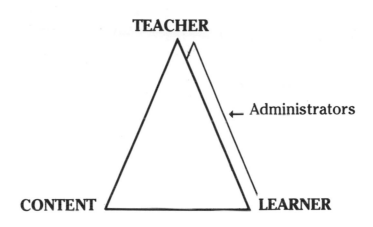

Parent Support Skills

Finally, we must consider the most critical sources of learning — the home and the community. As represented by parents or surrogates, the resources of the home must be directed to supporting the learning activities of the learners. Parent-support programs can be developed in much the same manner as can learner-management programs.

Recognizing the parents as learners, the teachers must use all of their teaching skills to facilitate the parents' involvement in learning-support programs. Recognizing the parents as teachers, the teachers must use all of their teaching skills to receive parent input and feedback, and to assist the parents in achieving their own teaching ends.

The teachers must focus upon the parents as supporters of learning. They must develop all of the support skills and knowledge programs necessary to enable the parents to support their children's learning. The teachers can do this by rotating their support programs through their teaching skills and incorporating the parent support skills necessary to make the teaching and learning skills work.

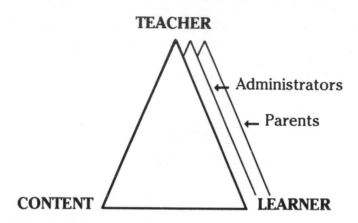

In summary, how we are able to involve the parents in supporting their children's learning will dictate how the children will, in their turn, parent their own children's learning.

TEACHER AS PERSON

The Benefits of Teaching

All of these responsibilities to others do not preclude the fact that teachers also benefit themselves in the teaching triangle. At each point, the teacher benefits personally.

As content developers, we have the opportunity to use our expertise to develop the *essential contribution* of our substance.

As planners, we have the opportunity to create a *whole new world of learning experiences*.

As learning managers, we have the opportunity to develop methods that manage *real learning*.

As programmers, we have the opportunity to make a *personal delivery* to another human being.

As helpers, we have the opportunity to come in *personal contact* with our learners.

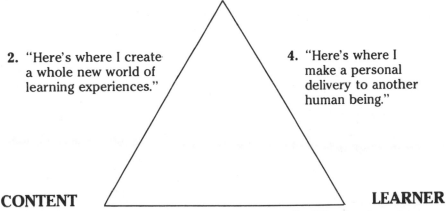

TEACHER
3. "Here's where I become a
real teacher by managing real
learning."

2. "Here's where I create
a whole new world of
learning experiences."

4. "Here's where I
make a personal
delivery to another
human being."

CONTENT

LEARNER

1. "Here's where I use my
expertise to develop
my contribution."

5. "Here's where I come
in personal contact
with my learners."

The Privileges of Effectiveness

Indeed, all of the functions, principles and benefits of the teaching triangle culminate in the development of the teacher as a person.

When we work with our content, we are *touching the substance of our contribution*. There are no greater privileges than to *know* something and to be able to *do* something.

When we use ourselves in transmitting the substance of our contribution, we are *coming in contact with ourselves*. We can only truly know ourselves through our behavior in relation to contributing to others.

When we transmit our contribution to others, we are *touching others*. We can only truly know others through their behavior at the moment of sharing a learning experience.

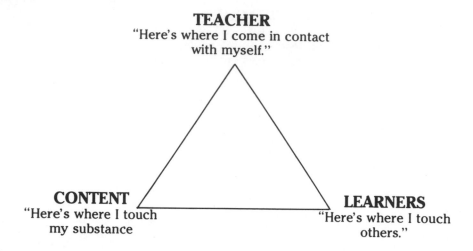

TEACHER
"Here's where I come in contact
with myself."

CONTENT
"Here's where I touch
my substance

LEARNERS
"Here's where I touch
others."

The Skilled Teacher - A Whole Person

For in the end, there are only ourselves, others and our substance. It matters – or not – that we lived only in these terms.

It is the use of our intellect in developing our substance that distinguishes us from all other forms of life. We are our substance.

It is only the self actualization of our human potential that rationalizes our existence for our seventy-odd years here on Earth. The only reason to live is to grow.

It is only our ability to touch others that enables the contributions of one generation to be passed on in refined forms by waves of succeeding generations. We live on past our years only in the contributions of those we have taught.

The TLC system may stand for "tender loving care" for humanity.

Only those who have truly touched others in a learning relationship know that we find God here on Earth in the other person.

RESEARCH BACKGROUND: SYSTEMS OF TEACHING

The Teaching-Learning System

The teaching and learning process that goes on in the classroom is a three-cornered process between teacher, learners and content. The skills that implement each of the interactions between these components constitute the skills of teaching.

The teaching and learning delivery system that goes on outside of the classroom is also a three-cornered process between: the school's delivery system; the learners' homes; and the communities, including business and government, that provide the general ecological context within which the learners function (Carkhuff and Becker, 1977).

In order to explore these relationships further we need to define what want our learners to look like. In other words, we want to define our learning products: our learners and what we want them to be able to do subsequent to teaching.

Model Systems

To do this there are several stages of system design in which we need to become involved (Friel and Carkhuff, 1980). First, we need to assess the contextual or environmental demands that will be made upon our learners in their living, learning and working environments. In other words, we need to assess the needs of learners in the different contexts within which they function. In so doing, we define our learner/products.

Second, we need to define these contextual or environmental demands in terms of definable outcomes: living, learning and working skill outcomes that are observable and measurable. In other words, we need to define the skill applications that our learners will make.

Third, we need to operationalize these outcomes. We need to define our living, learning and working skills outcomes as operational skill objectives with achievable skill steps and supportive knowledge. In other words, we need to define our skills content.

Fourth, we need to develop and deliver our skills content to our learners. In other words, we need to organize our content and teaching methods in a lesson plan and to make our delivery of the plan's content using our teaching delivery and interpersonal skills. In so doing, we are also effectively relating to the contextual variables from which the learners come and to which they will return.

Finally, having received the skills delivery, our learners will relate to the other variables: acquiring the skills by managing their own learning of the content; applying the skills to demonstrate the outcomes; and transferring the skills to their real life, living, learning and working contexts.

As can be seen, all variables relate to all other contiguous variables. Thus, the learners affect as well as they are affected by: the teachers, the content, the outcome, and the context. Similarly, each of the other variables operates to affect the variables contiguous to it.

In addressing these outcomes and processes, the models and systems of teaching are of limited value. All models translate their mission in terms of content objectives. However, only a few models focus programmatically upon the preparation of the skills and knowledge of the content by the teacher (Aspy and Roebuck, 1977; Bloom, et al, 1956; Kratwohl, 1964; Metfessel, Michael and Kirsner, 1969; Payne, 1968). Most models of teaching focus upon the teaching delivery between teacher and learners, calculated to accomplish one of three objectives: academic skills, for learning ways of dealing with intellectual complexities (Aspy and Roebuck, 1977; Ausubel, 1963; Bruner, Goodnow and Austin, 1967; Lorayne and Lucas, 1974; Piaget, 1952; Schwab, 1963; Sigel, 1969; Suchman, 1966; Sullivan, 1967; Taba, 1967); intrapersonal skills and knowledge, for individual problem-solving (Glasser, 1969; Gordon, 1961; Hunt, 1970; Perls, Hefferline and Goodman, 1977; Rogers, 1951, 1969; Schutz, 1967); or interpersonal skills and knowledge, for group problem-solving (Benne, Gibb and Bradford, 1964; Dewey, 1916; Massialas and Cox, 1966; Michaelis, 1963; Mosston, 1972; Schaftel and Schaftel, 1967; Thelen, 1960). However, few models of teaching are oriented toward the relationship of learners and content (Berenson, Berenson and Carkhuff, 1979;

Skinner, 1956; Wolpe, 1966). Fewer still are oriented toward the needs assessments of the contexts, and the definition of the outcomes (Carkhuff and Berenson, 1976; Friel and Carkhuff, 1980).

Model Programs

Perhaps the most dramatic model programs have been developed in an area that does not currently fall under the purview of public education: early childhood education (Bronfenbrenner, 1974). The principles derived from these programs may be stated in proposition form:

The most effective educational interventions are family-centered.

All evidence indicates that the family is the most effective and economical system for fostering and sustaining the development of the learners. Therefore, the involvement of the family as an active participant is critical to the success of any education program. Without such family involvement, any effects in the cognitive sphere erode very quickly once the program ends. The involvement of parents provides an on-going system which can not only reinforce the effects of the learning but also help to sustain them after the teaching program ends.

The most effective educational interventions are ecological interventions.

The most essential requirement is to provide those conditions that are necessary for life, and for the family to function as a childbearing and educational system. These include adequate health care, nutrition, housing, employment and parenthood. These are the conditions which are absent for the disadvantaged families around the world.

The most effective educational interventions are sequential.

A long-range education program must be viewed in terms of stages that are sequenced and continuous. If intervention is interrupted, gains are eroded. During every stage, the family's basic needs must be met first. Thereafter, intervention should be differentiated to accomodate the developmental level of both family and child, as indicated below:

1. Delivery Preparation – Preparation for parenthood and

childrearing where the parents control the central delivery function.

2. Delivery Functions – Where the parents are the primary source of effect in influencing the infant's early skills development.

3. Shared Delivery and Support Functions – Where the family and the educational system share responsibility for the early skills development of the child.

4. Support Functions – Where the school takes primary responsibility for delivery of skills, and the family takes responsibility for supporting skills development.

The results of these programs have been astounding, particularly when compared with those of traditional public education programs. For example, the work with severely disadvantaged children of mothers with IQ's below eighty is worth expanding upon (Heber, et al, 1971; Skeels, 1966; Skodak and Skeels, 1949). The basic design of these projects was to intervene in the early care of the children. Teacher-helpers stimulated and responded to the children and taught the mothers to do likewise. Substantial changes in the environments of the children and their principal caretakers produced positive developmental gains ranging from twenty-five to twenty-eight IQ points. From his own work, Aspy (1972) concludes that we can raise or lower the IQ of children as much as ten points per year, depending upon the nature of the intervention and the skills of the intervener or teachers. In addition, these changes are more enduring than those achieved by the most effective intervention techniques when the home is left essentially unaltered.

The principles found effective in the early childhood education programs are the principles that must come to dominate all educational programs. Those programs that are child-centered, age-segregated, time-bound, self-centered and focused exclusively on the trained professional as the most powerful and direct agent of intervention are doomed to fail. Those programs will succeed which: are family-centered rather than child-centered; cut across contexts, rather than being restricted to a single setting; have continuity over time; use as the primary agents of socialization the child's own family, peers, and school personnel who are part of the learner's enduring environment.

An Integrative Approach – A Summary

In summary, all helping and human relationships – and in particular, teaching – can have facilitative or retarding effects upon the recipients. The effects depend upon two sets of ingredients: the first, we may conceive of as skills development and delivery; the second, we may conceive of as a systems approach to education.

Skills Development

In terms of skills, the effects upon the learners are contingent upon the skills of their teachers. These teachers include informal, nonprofessionals as well as formal, professional teachers.

For the most part, the contributions of the nonprofessional teachers drawn from the family and community background are prepotent. They dominate because of the preponderance of time spent in these environments, certainly not because of the general level of their skill development. These effects also dominate because of the limited development of skills of those who are supposed to impact the learners – the teachers. In short, the effects of these nonprofessional teachers dominate because of time, and the essential neutrality of professional teachers.

The task, then, is to transform essentially neutral teachers into potent teachers, to equip them with the skills that potent teachers must possess, to make them "winners" instead of "losers."

Among others, the core of skills that potent teachers possess include the following: the ability to develop content to a skill objective (content development); the ability to organize content around a skill application (content organization); the ability to implement teaching methods emphasizing kinesthetic learning experiences (teaching methods); the ability to deliver the skills content in atomistic programs (teaching delivery); and the ability to relate to learners, and to individualize programs (interpersonal skills).

The effects of professional teachers, then, are contingent upon the level of development of their teaching skills. These skills enable them to develop and deliver their skills content in the classroom context of teacher, learners and content.

Systems Development

The effects of professional teachers are also dependent upon the level of development and interaction of the systems within which they function. These systems include the educational system; the home and family system; and the community-ecological system within which the home and family operates.

The educational system must first and foremost be responsible for the skills development of the teachers. The teachers must be skilled in order to make the skills delivery to the learners. In order to accomplish this function, the educational system must have organizational, program and personnel development components that are constantly processing the potential benefits of new systems and new technologies.

In turn, the teacher as well as the educational system must interact with the potent factors in the home and family environment, primarily people. There are many strategies for accomplishing this, including using the learners as intermediaries to maximize the learning of all parties involved, especially the learners. Most important, the people in the child-rearing systems must be educated to their different delivery and support roles, with regard to their children's development.

Finally, both the educational and child-rearing systems must relate to the community-ecological systems, including health care, nutrition, housing, and especially employment, thus directly involving business and government. These conditions are those necessary for survival, upon which the child's growth and development is predicated.

Again, the entire interaction of systems must be continuous and sequential in order to effect the individual delivery and support functions. At a molar level, for example, during the early development of the child, the child-rearing system has primary delivery responsibilities for the development of the child's living or socialization skills; the other systems serve to support this delivery function. At another developmental level, the educational system may have primary delivery responsibilities for the development of the child's learning skills; the other systems are supportive of this function. At a still later stage, the community-ecological system may have primary responsibilities for the development of the child's working skills; the other systems support.

In conclusion, if teachers want to account directly for more than five percent of the variance in their learners' achievement, they must do two things: they must develop the teaching skills that make them potent sources of effect; and they must contribute to developing and interacting with the educational, child-rearing and community-ecological systems that will allow the teachers to be potent sources of effect.

If teachers want to become effective, they must know themselves and insure their own growth.

If teachers want their learners to become effective, the teachers must know their learners and insure their growth.

If teachers want to become effective, they must become learners.

They must learn skills.

They must learn to interact with variables from the systems that now dominate learner achievement.

References

Aspy, D. N. *Toward A Technology for Humanizing Education.* Champaign, Ill.: Research Press, 1972.

Aspy, D. N. and Roebuck, Flora N. *KIDS Don't Learn From People They Don't Like.* Amherst, Mass.: Human Resource Development Press, 1977.

Ausubel, D. *Psychology of Meaningful Verbal Learning.* New York, N.Y.: Grune and Stratton, 1963.

Benne, K., Gibb, J. R. and Bradford, L. *T-Group Theory and Laboratory Method.* New York, N.Y.: Wiley, 1964.

Berenson, S. R., Berenson, D. H. and Carkhuff, R. R. *Learning Management Skills.* Amherst, Mass.: Carkhuff Institute of Human Technology, 1979.

Bloom, B. S., Englehart, M. D., Furst, E. J., Hill, W. H. and Kratwohl, D. R. *A Taxonomy of Educational Objectives: Handbook I, The Cognitive Domain.* New York, N.Y.: Longmans, Green, 1956.

Boocock, S. *Simulating Games in Learning.* Beverly Hills, Cal.: Sage Publications, 1968.

Bronfenbrenner, U. *A Report on Longitudinal Evaluations of Preschool Programs.* Washington, D.C.: DHEW, 1974.

Bruner, J., Goodnow, J. J. and Austin, G. A. *A Study of Thinking.* New York, N.Y.: Science Editions, Inc., 1967.

Carkhuff, R. R. and Becker, J. W. *Toward Excellence in Education.* Amherst, Mass.: Carkhuff Institute of Human Technology, 1977.

Carkhuff, R. R. and Berenson, B. G. *Teaching As Treatment.* Amherst, Mass.: Human Resource Development Press, 1976.

Dewey, J. *Democracy and Education.* New York, N.Y.: MacMillan, 1916.

Friel, T. W. and Carkhuff, R. R. *Training Systems Design.* Amherst, Mass.: Carkhuff Institute of Human Technology, 1980.

Glasser, W. *Schools Without Failure.* New York, N.Y.: Harper & Row, 1969.

Gordon, W. *Synectics.* New York, N.Y.: Harper & Row, 1961.

Heber, R., Garber, H., Harrington, S. and Hoffman, C. *Rehabilitation of Families at Risk for Mental Retardation.* Madison, Wis.: Rehabilitation Research and Training Center in Mental Retardation, University of Wisconsin, 1972.

Hunt, D. E. A. "Conceptual Level Matching Model for Coordinating Learner Characteristics with Educational Approaches," *Interchange, OISE Research Journal* 1.

Joyce, B. R. *Selected Learning Experiences.* Washington, D.C.: Association for Supervision and Curriculum Development, 1978.

Joyce, B. R. and Weil, M. *Models of Teaching.* Englewood Cliffs, N.J.: Prentice Hall, 1972.

Kratwohl, D. R. "The Taxonomy of Educational Objectives: Its Use in Curriculum Building," in *Defining Education Objectives,* Lindvall, C. M., ed. Pittsburgh, Pa.: University of Pittsburgh Press, 1964.

Lorayne, H. and Lucas, J. *The Memory Book.* New York, N.Y.: Ballantine, 1974.

Massialas, B. and Cox, B. *Inquiry in Social Studies.* New York, N.Y.: McGraw-Hill, 1966.

Metfessel, N.S., Michael, W. B. and Kirsner, D. A. "Instrumentation of Bloom's and Kratwohl's Taxonomies for the Writing of Educational Objectives," *Psychology in the Schools* 7 (3):227-231.

Michaelis, J. U. *Social Studies for Children in Democracy*. Englewood Cliffs, N.J.: Prentice Hall, 1963.

Mosston, M. *Teaching: From Command to Discovery*. Belmont, Cal.: Wadsworth Publishing Co., 1972.

Oliver, D. and Shaver, J. *Teaching Public Issues in the High School*. Boston, Mass.: Houghton Mifflin, 1966.

Payne, D. A. *The Specification and Measurement of Learning Outcomes*. Waltham, Mass.: Blaisdell Publishing Co., 1968.

Perls, F., Hefferline, R. and Goodman, P. *Gestalt Therapy: Excitement and Growth in the Human Personality*. New York, N.Y.: Crown, 1977.

Piaget, J. *The Origins of Intelligence in Children*. New York, N.Y.: International University Press, 1952.

Rogers, C. R. *On Becoming a Person*. Boston, Mass.: Houghton Mifflin, 1951.

Rogers, C. R. *Freedom to Learn*. Columbus, Ohio: Merrill, 1969.

Schaftel, F. and Schaftel, G. *Role-Playing for Social Values: Decision-Making in the Social Studies*. Englewood Cliffs, N.J.: Prentice Hall, 1967.

Schutz, W. Joy. *Expanding Human Awareness*. New York, N.Y.: Grove Press, 1967.

Schwab, J. J. *Biology Teacher's Handbook*. New York, N.Y.: Wiley, 1965.

Sigel, I. E. "The Piagetian System and the World of Education," in *Studies in Cognitive Development*, D. Elkind and J. Flavell, eds. New York, N.Y.: Oxford, 1969.

Index

Author Index